Young Playwrights 101

a practical guide for young playwrights
and those who teach them

Jonathan Dorf

YouthPlays Press

Cover art by Neil K. Scott.
Cover and Writer's Web design by Jonathan Snipes.

ISBN 1-59971-069-2

Acknowledgements

Thanks to Matt Buchanan for his invaluable feedback as my de facto editor, and for his contribution to the section about sets and staging.

Thanks to Leon Katz, for his inspiration and ability to bring bolts of clarity out of the blue when they were needed most.

Thanks to William Alfred, my first great playwriting mentor. I miss you, and I hope that Chance is making Tinker and Evers proud.

Thanks to Ed Shockley, my longtime friend and colleague, for his boundless energy and his seemingly endless supply of new ways to look at our craft.

Thanks to Andria Biblioni and Chris Fox at The Haverford School and Athena Schultz at The Writers Store.

Thanks to the many who have taught me much over the years, whose lessons and insights have found their way into the book in one way or the other: Velina Hasu Houston, Edit Villarreal, Hanay Geiogamah, Tony Kubiak, Bob Brustein, Greg Gunter, Jeff Sweet, Adrienne Kennedy and especially to Thom Williams, who encouraged me to write my first play.

And above all, thanks to my parents, who are indispensable.

TABLE OF CONTENTS

Introduction

Imagine a dark theater. The lights come up. An actor walks onstage. The audience sits on the edge of its collective seat, waiting to see what will happen. What will he say? What will she do? And there you are, sitting in the back of the house, watching the audience watch the actors perform your words and carry out the actions you wrote. You're the playwright, and there is no greater thrill than sitting in the back of that dark theater watching your work being performed on a live stage.

Of course, arriving at that moment of triumph takes a lot of work, and if you've never written a play, it can seem like pretty scary stuff. How do you start? That's where this book comes in. I created *Young Playwrights 101* specifically for young writers and those who teach them. If you follow the chapters in order, it's designed to be a complete playwriting course that will guide you from "wire to wire" in the creation of a new play. It works equally well whether you're a complete beginner, or you've written plays before and simply want to pick up some pointers. In each chapter you'll find lessons and tips about different elements of playwriting, and that instruction, when appropriate, is followed by writing exercises to allow you to practice what you've learned. Of course, if you're just looking for help with specific elements in your writing, feel free to go right to the help you need.

Ready to begin? Act I, Scene 1…lights up.

Chapter 1

GETTING STARTED

What Is a Play?

Everybody knows what a play is. Right? You'd be surprised.

Sure—we all agree that *Hamlet* or *Romeo and Juliet* is a play, but what many people think of as plays are really "skits." What's the difference? Some years back, *Saturday Night Live* had a very funny scene on an airplane, where as each passenger was getting off the plane, the flight attendant said "buh bye." No matter what the passenger said or tried to say, the response was the same: "Buh bye." It was funny, but it was nothing more than a clever concept that went nowhere. No one changed, and no story developed: it was a skit.

A play, on the other hand, has a beginning, middle and end. It goes somewhere, even if that place is, in the case of the Samuel Beckett masterpiece *Waiting for Godot*, right back where it started.

Plays, of course, come in all shapes and sizes. Some are only a minute long (in fact, there are competitions for these short-shorts), whereas others, like the Pulitzer Prize-winning *Kentucky Cycle* by Robert Schenkkan, can last six hours or longer. In recent years, ten-minute plays have become very popular (probably as a result of the big Actors Theatre of Louisville competition), and one-act plays are always in demand at schools and community theatres for festivals and competitions (e.g. Thespians). And then there are musicals, which require not only someone to write the book (i.e. the story and any dialogue), but also lyrics and music.

All of this can be bewildering. Where do you begin? You may have huge stories you want to tell, stories full of passion and emotion. There is often a lot happening to you as you grow up, and the stories you want to tell express that. The problem is that—at least for most of us—it usually takes a little while for our playwriting "chops" to catch up with our ideas. No worries—with hard work, you'll get there. But start small.

There's another important reason not to try to write the next *Hamlet* or *Rent* for your first play: you want to be able to finish it. Not finishing is a big problem for writers of all ages, but it's a particularly big problem for the new/young writer, because when you're just starting out, you don't necessarily have a big bag of tricks to get you through. All right—*Hamlet* and *Rent* are out. Then what's in?

My favorite way to begin is with a ten-minute play, which, at roughly a page per minute, should be no more than ten pages long (in fact, most ten-minute play contests have made this length limit a rule). It's got a beginning, middle and an end, only everything happens more quickly.

You might be surprised at how many theatres look specifically for ten-minute pieces, though you really shouldn't be. Ten-minute festivals have sprung up all over the place, because they allow a theatre to produce lots of new plays without much financial risk and to get more people involved (think of how many actors can participate!). That means more people whose friends will come, which means a crowded theatre and decent box office. Everybody wins.

But don't think of a ten-minute play as any less of a play than a longer one. It's not. Ten-minute plays can be powerful, exciting, amazing. Think of them as the haiku of the playwriting world. I still write at least one a year. Their big advantage over longer plays? They're easier to finish, and you have a much better chance of getting one produced than a full-length play. And after all, we don't write plays to have them sit in a drawer or on a computer hard drive. We write them to be produced and have them go out into the world to affect people. Once you write a few ten-minute plays, you can write a one-act of more substantial length and eventually work your way up to a full-length. But it's not about one type of play being superior to another. Each is its own art form.

Where Ideas Come From

Before you can write a play, you need something to write about: you need an idea.

Ideas come from anywhere and everywhere. Here are some possibilities to get you started:

A line of dialogue or overheard conversation. Maybe you hear a few words in your head, or perhaps someone says something in the school parking lot that catches your attention. Who said it? Why?

A title. Sometimes titles come to us before the actual plays do. For example, I have a play called *Last Right Before the Void*. The title came first—it was my way of describing the directions to a particular theater where one of my plays was being performed. From there, I fleshed out the play, which ended up being about a young man hitchhiking on a highway that seemed to disappear into nowhere.

A character, either one you've made up or one based on someone you have met or observed or read about. This is perhaps the most common seed for a play. Who is this person? What does she want? Who else is in her world?

A historical event. Many plays are in some way connected to events that happened in history. It doesn't have to be a major event, and, in fact, sometimes the most interesting plays are ones that are based on events that few people know about, or deal with more obscure moments in better-known events (e.g. some little-known incident in World War I).

A place. Perhaps a kind of place comes to mind, like an office or a classroom or a playground. Or it could be a specific one, like the

Chapter 2

CHARACTERS AND CONFLICT

Models for Building Characters

You can't have a play without characters. You can put talking (or non-talking) dogs or rocks on stage, but guess what: in their own way, they're still characters. That means you have to figure out who they are. Let me suggest three possible models:

Model One
This is sometimes called the police file or bone structure model, and it's the most detailed. Start by dividing a character's attributes into three categories: physical, social and psychological.

Physical pertains to a person's body, and for the most part, these are things we know just by looking at him. Examples: gender, age, height, weight, skin color, hair color and texture, eye color, build (i.e. muscularity), health (e.g. general wellness, diseases, etc.)...

Social has to do with a person and her place in society. Examples: education, class (i.e. social class, as in upper, middle or lower), job, hobbies, personal history, family background, living situation, religion...

Psychological has to do with a person's emotional and intellectual make-up. Examples: intelligence, temperament, fears and phobias, ambitions...

Be as thorough as you can in creating the character, but remember that not all (maybe not even most) of this information will find its way into the play. So why bother to make it up? Isn't it a waste of time? The answer is no, because this information will help you get to know a character and give you ideas about her behavior. For example, knowing that Ellen's childhood best friend was black may push Ellen to stick up for a black woman she doesn't know in a dispute at a restaurant. That Ellen's friend was black may never come up in the play, but you, the author, know.

Model Two
This is the opposite extreme from the police file model: just start writing. Create an age and gender for your character, then let him behave how he wants to behave. This is probably best for experienced writers, because it requires you to have a strong built-in sense of character development and storytelling structure.

Model Three
This is the compromise between Models One and Two, but that doesn't mean it's a compromise in quality. Come up with the character's name and gender, then try to create a few defining points for each character. For example, Ben, the homeless teen and title character from the play I mentioned earlier, was put up for adoption when he was nearly four years old, used to wrestle before he dropped out of high school and was abused by his therapist. He is nearly sixteen years old. These pieces of information define, in broad strokes, who he is and why he does many of the things he does. The details can then come in the writing. I like this approach because it gives you a foundation, but it doesn't lock you in. This is how I work.

Model Three "A"
This is a slightly more structured variation on Model Three. For each character, come up with three words to describe him. For example, he is a son, a student and a skateboarder. Come up with three physical characteristics (e.g. athletic) and three emotional ones (e.g. afraid of heights) to go along with them. Add in one problem: he wants to buy a car. Find an obstacle: he has no money. Sprinkle one secret into the mix: he lives under a fake name because his parents are illegal immigrants—and you're ready to serve.

Still Having Trouble? Find a Verb

If you're still having a hard time getting a handle on your character, try this tip: define each character with a verb, and let that verb help you shape the character's behavior. For example, the verb for Steffi may be "to hide." That verb dictates how Steffi operates. It might mean that she leaves the room rather than have a confrontation, or that she doesn't travel without her friend (behind whom she hides).

EXERCISE: Character Builder

Build a character using the models described above. Begin with Model Three, then Model Three A, and finally Model One (we'll skip Model Two, because there's really not much to do with it). You can either use the same character for each build, or different ones. In either case, you'll notice that we're moving from less detailed to more. Try these different character creation models on for size and see what fits most comfortably.

Do I Have to Develop Every Character?

The answer is no—at least not too much. Sometimes a character is there merely to fulfill a particular function. For example, a teacher may be in the play to hand out a detention, or a guard may be there to show that there is security at the office building, or a messenger, even if she brings some crucial document, may just be in the play to deliver that document (though make sure, if you have a character who is only there for one reason, that you absolutely need her in the play). We don't need to know every character's life story, but every major character should have at least some basic development. As a rule of thumb, the more a character appears on stage, the more development you'll want to do. Of course, this doesn't mean that a character that only appears once, for example, isn't important. In fact, in a play like Henrik Ibsen's *Ghosts*, the dead Captain Alving looms so powerfully over the others that he's the greatest force in the play, even though he never appears at all.

Developing a Character Who Isn't On Stage…

So how do I learn more about someone that I can't even see? It's not as difficult as it might seem. One way for the offstage person to come up is in the dialogue of the other characters. For example, imagine two employees at a jewelry store having a conversation. We catch a sliver of dialogue.

FIRST EMPLOYEE
Don't touch that—you know how Mr. Simmons walks around with that darn magnifying glass.

Already, we know that Mr. Simmons is someone to be feared and/or respected (they call him Mister even when he's not around, and they're concerned about how he might react), and that he's incredibly meticulous (to use a magnifying glass). We can imply that he's using it to check up on them.

Rather than have one character tell us everything about this offstage character all at once, better to give us bits and pieces, slowly building a picture and our anticipation of meeting this person—if we ever do. Using an object that belongs to the absent character is another good technique. Maybe Mr. Simmons has left his coat ominously hanging on a hook by the door, and the employees are both too afraid to move it. Or maybe there's a nameplate on a desk or a door that marks his "presence."

Behave!

For all of the background work and set-up we do, characters are still about behavior: what they do. Sometimes the answer to why a character does what she does is "because she does." If everyone behaved exactly how we expect them to all the time, that wouldn't make for an interesting play, would it? So remember to keep the focus on what your characters do.

Characters, Practically Speaking

All this talk about characters brings up an important practical question: how many characters should my play have? The answer is as many as you need to tell the story, but let's be practical. If you're writing for the professional theatre, four to six actors (maybe eight, but it's a stretch) is the maximum that most companies will hire these days. (Remember, even an actor with only one line needs to be paid.) Of course, there are professional companies that will produce plays with larger casts, but they are a minority.

Some professional companies produce plays that are specifically written to tour to schools or similar venues. Chances are you've had one visit your school. My *From Shakespeare With Love?* was just such a play, and the Walnut Street Theatre toured it around the Philadelphia area. It had a cast of four, which tends to be the maximum for this type of show. In fact, you'll see a number of these touring productions in which there are only one or two actors.

On the other hand, schools usually want larger cast plays (with lots of female or gender-flexible roles) so that they can use more students. Community theatres tend to be more like schools in their desire for larger casts. Does that mean you have to choose between satisfying the needs of professional theatres (small cast) or school/community theatres (large cast)? Sometimes you do. But one way around this is to allow for the option of multiple casting, in which the same actor plays more than one character. That way, if a group wants to use only a few actors, each actor can play multiple roles, but if they want to use more actors, they can have actors play a single (or at least fewer) roles. For example, in *Now You See Me*, one actor can play Joanne, Jenn's Friend, June, the Second TV Personality and the Third New Friend—or five different actors can cover those roles.

There is one big, huge, gigantic element of character that I haven't mentioned yet. In mathematics, the difference between speed and velocity is direction. Characters in your play don't exist in a vacuum. They have direction, and that direction is the thing they want. That want could be something material (money in Joe Orton's *Loot*) or something more abstract, for example wanting to feel valued and productive, like Willy Loman in Arthur Miller's *Death of a Salesman*. But whatever it is—and we'll talk more about this when we get to conflict later—it has to be something important, something worth going after with all of the resources at the character's disposal.

Does every character have to want something? The character at the cash register of the bakery who is only there to ring up the sale probably doesn't need to, but every major character should have some kind of want. Of course, the problem with having a strong want is that, if you're not careful, it can make your character one-dimensional. So after the set of character development exercises below, stay tuned for a lesson that will help with that, something called the **Tension of Opposites**…

EXERCISES: Character Development

Below are a series of exercises designed to work your character development muscles.

1. Pick a person on the street and turn him into a character by asking questions. Who is he? Where is he coming from? What does he want? Perhaps he has just come from making a major change in his life: what is it?

2. Write a few sentences about either your first character or a new character:
>   Happiest day of the character's life.
>   Biggest fear.
>   Biggest disappointment.
>   Thing she wants most.

3. A day in the life of your character.

4. An embarrassing childhood moment.

5. A "first" for the character (e.g. first job, first time sleeping away from home, etc.).

Tension of Opposites

When I was writing *Shining Sea*, the legendary Leon Katz was my dramaturg (an advisor and constructive critic for the playwright during the writing/rehearsal process). Pac, one of the characters, is so named because he's obsessed with the Pacific Ocean. He's never been there, but he'll do anything to get there. On the one hand, it's a very clear want. The problem is that it started to make Pac one-dimensional.

Leon's suggestion was to give Pac some other strong pull or desire that creates tension with his primary want. This "tension of opposites" —the second item isn't necessarily a literal opposite (just different enough from their primary want)—instantly gives a character dimension and inner tension. In Pac's case, I gave him pets he loved: rats. Suddenly, he wasn't just trying to get to the Pacific, but also trying to make a good home and ensure the safety of his beloved rats. It filled Pac out as a character.

Not every character will have this problem, but if you run into one who needs more depth and dimension, the tension of opposites can be a good way to give it to him.

Conflict

Now that you've created characters, given them strong wants and filled them out, it's time to create conflict. Conflict is when characters' wants are in opposition. I want the ball, you want the same ball, and we both want it so badly that neither of us is willing to compromise. Not only that, but if we don't get what we want, something truly awful is going to happen to us.

This "something truly awful is going to happen to us" is called having something at stake, or simply the stakes. If nothing happens to me if I don't get the ball, then no matter how much I may say I need it, I really don't. Obviously, the highest stakes are life or death, and the closer you can get to those, the better. Not every play can be a life or death struggle, of course, but try to find the highest stakes you can that make sense for your characters. It might be a character faced with losing his job or being expelled from school or having to give up a child...anything that makes your character willing to dig in and fight.

One important byproduct of characters being totally committed to getting what they want and having something crucial at stake is that they're not likely to compromise. Why not? Two reasons. One, if you need something that badly, you're not going to turn around all of a sudden and at least partly give it up. Two, if you've been battling it out for an entire play with another character, it's not believable that you're both suddenly going to play nice and give in. You've fought too long and hard for what you want, and you probably don't like each other much by this point. If it's possible for you both to compromise, why couldn't you have done that at the beginning and saved us from having to sit through the play?

One way to enhance the conflict is by using what I call the "ticking time bomb." Setting it up is simple enough: give the characters a limited time in which to resolve the conflict or the bomb goes off. For example, if George loves Martha, but Martha is going to be married to Sam on Thursday, then George only has until Thursday to stop the wedding. If he doesn't, the bomb goes off: he loses Martha. This is a technique used effectively in film as well. Think of *Star Wars*: if the rebels don't destroy the Death Star before it becomes fully operational, it will destroy them.

There are two other important elements to conflict that beginning writers often miss. The first is that the characters you create need to be strong, strong enough to hold their own against the others. A weak character will get steamrolled by an adversary and can't sustain a play. Think of the classic Greek play *Antigone* by Sophocles. While Creon may be the man in power and is ultimately likely to get his way, Antigone is strong enough in her convictions and her resourcefulness to be a match for him, thus keeping the play engaging.

The second problem that often troubles new writers (and sometimes not so new writers) is not understanding that argument and

Sydney Opera House or the Oval Office. What sort of characters would be in that place? What might they be doing there?

Newspapers and magazines. News stories are great inspiration for writers, as are **photographs**. It doesn't even have to be a major story, nor do you have to use the actual characters involved. Perhaps a clipping about a missing elephant from the zoo or a photo from a celebrity wedding is enough to give you an idea. I once saw a picture of Newt Gingrich, then Speaker of the US House of Representatives, speaking at ®Boys Town, the home for boys (and now girls as well) made famous by the movie starring Spencer Tracy, who won an ®Oscar for his role. That became the seed for my ten-minute play *Newt Gingrich Visits a Residential Youth Facility Not Near Omaha*.

Other sources of inspiration could come from **paintings**, **music**, **famous sayings** or **expressions, titles** (of books, songs, poems, etc.) or **objects** (perhaps some particular food, for example). The possibilities are endless.

Be careful about using **television shows** or **movies,** though, for inspiration. Yes, it's tempting to make up your own version of *Survivor* or *X-Men*, but someone already wrote those, and not only is it not very creative to borrow their characters or stories, it's usually against the law. The one exception is in the case of parody (a very specific type of comedy that makes fun of the original work), but wouldn't you rather come up with your own idea?

There is such a thing as an **adaptation**, which is when a playwright takes another source (usually a **book**) and turns it into a play. The Broadway musical *Cats* is an adaptation of T.S. Eliot's *Old Possum's Book of Practical Cats* (a collection of poetry), and such novels as *The Grapes of Wrath*, *Of Mice and Men*, *Little Women* and *The Chosen* have all been successfully adapted to the stage. Shaw's *Pygmalion*, a non-musical play, later became the basis for the musical *My Fair Lady*. Before you consider doing an adaptation, though, there are some important things you need to know, both from a writing standpoint and from a legal one. I'll discuss them in Chapter 7.

One other source of inspiration that requires careful handling is the
"**theme**" or "**issue**" (or "**cause**"). It's certainly noble to want to write
plays that raise awareness or even change people's minds about major
issues in our lives, but the danger is that when you start a play with an
agenda, it ends up not being a play: it can become preachy and one-
dimensional, more like an essay pretending to be a play. Not a good
thing.   Having said that, when I was playwright-in-residence at
Choate Rosemary Hall, the first summer I was there wasn't that long
after the Columbine massacre, and after talking to the students, I
wrote a play about school violence called *Now You See Me*. To avoid
falling into the trap I just warned you about, I made sure the play was
about the characters and their story. If it's done well, your audience
will "get it."   Mixing in some comedy helps, too (though writing
funny isn't necessarily easy). So if you must write about an issue, be
sure you write about people—trust that the issue will be there in your
characters' stories.

EXERCISE: Twenty Seeds

This is a very simple exercise. Every idea is a seed for a play. Your
job is to come up with twenty seeds from which a play could grow,
using the above categories (or ones of your own) for inspiration.
Don't worry about planting your seeds yet—just gather the
ingredients for your garden.

Write What You Know—Or Not?

Many young writers (and older ones) are told, "Write what you
know." On the surface, it sounds like good advice. Can't write what
you don't know about. Very sensible. The problem is that as a young
writer, you haven't lived that long, so your experiences are limited.
You haven't been married or divorced or had to pay the rent or the
mortgage or be the one counted upon to put food on the table. Unless
you're very lucky, you probably haven't traveled all that much, and
hopefully you haven't seen too much misery out in the world. So
does that mean you're not allowed to write about any of those things?
Are you limited to writing plays about teens and your own limited

experiences? Why write what you know when what you don't know is so much more interesting?

You do, however, have an obligation to learn about what you don't know, so that you can write about it honestly. For example, I wrote a play, *Ben*, about a teenager living on the street in Harvard Square, looking for the woman he believes is his mother. How much of this world did I know? I lived in Harvard Square during college and was a teenager at one time, but I've never been homeless and have two wonderful parents whom I've known since birth. In other words, the life of this teenager, Ben, was not one I had experienced. So I educated myself about it. I read books about homelessness and street youth, and I spent a semester volunteering at a shelter for troubled teens. I kept my eyes open when I walked around the Square, observing the teens who hung out in the area they called "the Pit." By the time I started writing, it may not have been a world in which I had lived, but it was certainly one with which I was familiar.

Most of us will never, for example, be an astronaut. But if we do our homework, we can create a character who's an astronaut, or write about what it's like to be one.

EXERCISE: Research

Pick a character with a job with which you're not familiar. Come up with a minimum of three details about the character's life in that job, using either reading or a first-person interview to get your information. Do NOT use film or television as your source of information. For example, if you decide to pick a teacher, you might learn that she is paid bi-weekly on the second and fourth Fridays of the month, that she is in her classroom by 7:00 AM every day for extra help sessions, and that she is issued a laptop by the school, but that no personal files are allowed to be stored on it. There are countless other details ripe for the picking...

I Have an Idea: Now What?

Once you have an idea, it's time to play "what if?" In other words, you're going to take your idea and run with it.

For example, let's say our inspiration is a baseball. What if that baseball belonged to a boy who believed it was the only thing responsible for his good luck? What if someone took it? What would he do to get it back? From the seed of a baseball, a play begins to grow.

Or what if our play begins around the famous phrase "I have not yet begun to fight," credited to John Paul Jones, captain of the American ship *Bonhomme Richard*, during his confrontation with the British warship *Serapis* during the American Revolutionary War—only this time, what if it's said by one girl baking cookies to another? What if they're competing in the local Little Miss Baking Queen pageant? What if their mothers are even more concerned with who wins than they are? A comedy is definitely ready to sprout from this seed of a line of dialogue.

EXERCISE: What If?

Taking the seeds you came up with in Twenty Seeds, it's time to ask "what if?" Choose your five favorites (or any five) and see if, for each one, you can develop the same kind of three or four sentence progression that I did for "I have not yet begun to fight." Perhaps you'll like one or more of these seeds enough to want to grow them into plays.

Having an idea and asking "what if?" is the first step toward creating the world of your play. But who lives in this world? It's time to build some characters.

disagreement are not the same thing as conflict. For example, we can argue about which is the better baseball team: I like the Philadelphia Phillies, while you like the New York Yankees. But no matter what the outcome of the argument, there is nothing at stake for either of us if we lose. On the other hand, if our family has only one car and we're arguing over who gets to take it tonight—I need it for work and you need it for a date—then we're in conflict. We both want something, and we both have something to lose if we don't get what we want. Having something at stake, something important, is what separates conflict from mere argument or disagreement.

EXERCISE: Conflict or Argument?

First, decide whether each situation below is already a conflict, or whether it's just an argument. If it's an argument, how could it be turned into a conflict?

1. Zack's rabbit is a much better pet than Melissa's Labrador.

2. We should have peanut butter and jelly for lunch, not steak.

3. I want to replace you as starting goalie of the soccer team.

4. I want you to give back the jacket you borrowed.

5. Your hair is brown. You keep telling me it's red.

Chapter 3

SETTING

Now that you've created all these really great characters, you have to put them somewhere at a particular time.

The Where Part I: Theater Spaces

Settings in plays don't exist in a vacuum: they exist in a physical theater space. So before you make a decision about the setting for your play, it makes sense to know about the different kinds of theater spaces in which it might be produced.

Sometimes you know that a particular theatre group (or your school) is going to produce your play before you write it. For example, maybe there is a school one-act festival, and if they select your entry, you know that it will be produced in the auditorium. In my case, I had several commissions (a commission is when a theatre company or other group pays you to write a play for them to produce) at the Choate Rosemary Hall Summer Arts Conservatory, so I knew exactly where they were going to stage *Now You See Me*, for example, at the end of the summer.

More often, however, we don't know where a play will be produced, and even if it's produced first in one venue, we of course hope that it will be produced in many, many other places later on. A few thoughts to guide you:

- Different types of spaces have advantages and disadvantages. (We'll talk about them in a moment.)

- Your play may work better in one type of space than another—and that's all right. Many plays have a "best" space—it doesn't mean that they won't work just fine in other types of spaces if they have to.

- Because you want your play to be produced as widely as possible, you'll want to think very carefully before writing a play that cannot be produced in a particular type of space (usually because of set/design requirements).

And now, on to the types of theater spaces...

Proscenium
Since the proscenium is by far the most common type of stage, you will probably want your play to work well in this configuration—which typically isn't too hard, because it's what we're used to seeing anyway. The proscenium (the archway at the front of the stage) separates the actors and the world of the play from the audience. Often, the stage is raised, though sometimes instead of the stage being raised, the house (where the audience sits) is raised, meaning that the further back you go, the higher the seats. This is known as a rake.

The proscenium (except in the case of a black box when it's set up like a proscenium) is the only one of the major types of theater spaces in which you can have a traditional "box set": a set with three walls and a missing "fourth wall" open to the audience. Or, if you'd like to use multiple sets and scenes, a proscenium is well-suited to that, though you're still limited by your budget (more sets cost more money) and by the time that it takes to change sets in the middle of a play. But at least there's no design/staging reason why you can't have those multiple sets, which is not necessarily true of the other spaces. Read on to find out why...

Thrust
In a thrust configuration, which is relatively rare at the school (or indeed any) level, the playing area extends (i.e. thrusts) into the

audience area, so the actors have audience on three sides of them. In other words, there's nothing separating the two groups (no "picture frame," as people sometimes describe the proscenium archway) to create a feeling of "us" (the audience) and "them" (the actors). Obviously, this creates a more intimate setting—if you're in the audience, the action is happening immediately in front of you.

The drawback with thrust is that you have less flexibility with your scenery. You can have a wall or backdrop at the back of the stage, but the rest of your scenery must be designed so that it doesn't block anyone's view. Typically, productions will use set pieces (i.e. furniture) or treat the floor to create different rooms or areas. For example, a sofa and a coffee table might create the living room, while part of the stage floor might be painted green or have fake turf to designate the lawn area. (Thrust houses usually have steep rakes so that the audience can actually see the floor.) Also, since any scene changes will have to take place in plain view of the audience, thrust productions are usually played on a unit set: a single unified structure that remains on the stage throughout the play, with few (if any) changes made to it. More on the unit set in **The Where: Part II**. The bottom line is that if you can keep your scenic requirements in check, thrust can be a great way to create a more "up close and personal" feel to your play.

In the Round
In this playing situation, also relatively rare compared to the proscenium, the actors have audience on all sides of them, and entrances and exits are through the audience (there are aisles, of course).

Plays set in the round have even less scenic flexibility than thrust productions. Basically, any piece of scenery more than a few feet high will somehow have to be "see thru," or it will block any actor who moves behind it—and because the actors have audience members on every side, every spot on stage is "behind it" from the point of view of at least one member of the audience. Want to do a realistic interior with three walls, like that box set we mentioned in the discussion of the proscenium? No can do in the round, because most of your audience will be stuck staring at a wall instead of your actors.

The in the round setting also forces the director to work harder when staging the play. An actor cannot stand in one place for a long period of time, delivering a monologue or having a conversation, because he needs to give everyone in the audience his front. If you know you are writing for this kind of space, it is a good idea to avoid long seated conversations, or any situation that would prevent an actor from "working the room." So why would anyone want to perform plays in the round? Theatre in the round has a wonderful sense of theatricality about it. Since everyone in the audience can see others in the audience across the stage, the event takes on an energized, almost circus-like atmosphere that can serve some plays very well.

Black Box
This is the most flexible set-up (and the easiest space for which to write), because the stage and the house together form a large rectangle or square, and the playing and seating areas can be configured in any way the director wishes. In other words, a black box can become any of the other major types of theater spaces. Or it can become something totally unique: I once saw a production in which the audience members sat on swings hanging from the ceiling throughout the space, and the actors played among them. Anything is possible, but remember that if you want your play to be produced all over, as I said before, you'll want to make sure it can work in a wide variety of spaces, including the traditional ones.

Now that you have an idea about the types of theater spaces, it's time to turn your attention to what to put in them...

The Where Part II: Types of Sets

As a playwright, it pays to be set-sensible, so keep a few basics in mind. For example, the more you have to build, the more it costs and the longer it takes. Just as important, if you have to make a major set change during the performance, it takes time. Don't write a play that forces the audience to sit in the dark for two minutes while the running crew scampers on and changes the set, because no amount of cool music will hide the fact that the audience is sitting in the dark for two minutes waiting for a set change. If you must have a major set change, try to write it so that it can be done during intermission, or write into the script something that will cover it. For example, one possible solution is to stage a scene in front of the curtain while a set change is going on behind it. Of course, not every theater has a curtain …

Now that we've gotten that out of the way, what are your set options?

Unit Set
For the longest time, this has been the most common type of set at the school level. The stage crew gets together, and they build one set that sits there for the entire performance. Considering how often schools trot out such old chestnuts as *Arsenic and Old Lace* (Kesselring), the unit set is often a living room or other interior space (usually the box set mentioned earlier). To have a unit set, it means that your play has only one setting.

Multiple Sets
This means exactly what it says: there is more than one set in the play. How a production handles this, however, is another matter. It could mean that they build multiple fully realized sets (which means that you have the issue of changing them either between scenes or at intermission), or that they use suggested sets...

Suggested Sets
When a play uses suggested sets, it means that instead of a full set for each setting, each different place is only hinted at. For example, a couch might suggest a living room. A kitchen might be defined by a kitchen table and some chairs. A forest might be accomplished almost completely with lighting (you can buy a tree gobo for a few dollars). Personally, I'm a big fan of suggested sets. Why? Because if you don't want to write a play that stays in one place the entire time, using suggested sets makes it possible for someone to produce your play without spending a great deal of money on the sets, or spending a great deal of time changing them during the show. True, it means that your stage crew doesn't get the joy of playing with power tools and swinging hammers at some monster set that sprawls across the stage, but at the same time, there's a great opportunity to be

creative in the way you suggest a beach or a classroom or a doctor's office.

Even if you really, really want your play to be done on a turntable with five completely built sets that rotate with the click of a button, since that's not likely to happen, it's a good idea to write directly into the script that it's OK to use suggested sets. Don't leave it for your reader to come to this conclusion on his own.

One staging technique often used with suggested sets, or with a play that has multiple settings, is to divide the stage into playing areas. That way, rather than moving things on and off, the characters move to a different place on stage. Sometimes called Elizabethan staging, I suggest using it in *War of the Buttons*: the abandoned ice cream factory would be in one place, the boarding school dorm in another, and still other parts of the stage would be the grocery store and Ticker's living room. It helps keep the play moving.

Or what if everything in your play occurs in one place, except for one scene? Maybe you really want a unit set, but this one scene is tripping you up. First, ask yourself if that scene is truly necessary, and if it has to take place in a different setting. If it does and you still want a unit set, you might consider using a special area for that one scene, perhaps out in front (i.e. downstage) of the unit set. If you think creatively, there is almost always a way to solve any set issue.

Before we completely depart the land of theater spaces and sets, there is one special case: the touring play, which I mentioned briefly in the discussion about cast size in **Characters, Practically Speaking**. I'm not talking, of course, about *Rent* or *The Lion King* or other similar "Broadway-style" national tours, but rather about plays that tour to schools and similar venues. For example, let's say you write a play about alcohol abuse or Mark Twain or Thanksgiving that will be put on at all of the elementary schools in your district. Because the play has to travel, you need to be able to pack up your set and props, fit them into a trunk (like the one you use for summer camp) and put the trunk in the back of somebody's minivan. So in this case, you'll need to be extremely creative about devising a minimal, suggested set that can travel and be produced in any space, which might even be a crowded classroom.

The Where Part III: Choosing Your Wheres

Now that we know about the kinds of venues where your play could be produced and the set options, it's time to get down to business: where is your play going to happen? Where are all these characters you've created with such care going to live? Not all settings are created equal. The setting that works best for your play is the one that allows you to create the most conflict and tension when you put your characters in it. For example, it's more exciting for an escaped prisoner to be hiding in a police station than in a remote forest. Ditto a suicidal person on a ledge rather than in a psychiatrist's office, or a young actor with stage fright on a stage instead of telling a friend about it in the cafeteria.

EXERCISE: Find the Tension

Given these characters and their situations, suggest a setting that would create strong tension:

1. An alcoholic who is desperately trying to quit drinking.
2. A woman who can't swim and is afraid of the water.
3. Two claustrophobics.
4. A pair of cheerleaders competing for the last spot on the roster.
5. A thief with a stolen painting.

Setting Tip: Take a Walk!

Noted playwright and screenwriter Bruce Graham told a group of us sitting around a conference table one morning in Philadelphia that he likes to walk around his settings. For example, when he was going to write about characters in a hotel, he checked into a hotel and explored. What kind of rooms are there? What activities happen there? What characters exist in that space? What props might be lying around? What makes a hotel setting unique and different from a private home or an apartment building? Is the hotel a high-rise? Modern or more old-fashioned? What state of repair is it in? So if you're going to write about characters at school, even though you may go there every day, pay a visit to your school as a playwright—you may see things differently than you do as a student.

EXERCISE: Inventory

This exercise goes with the **Take a Walk!** tip above. Take a walk around your school or another potential setting of your choice. Observe as many details as possible about the setting, including notes about the rooms, objects you find there, people you find there. Try to come up with at least a dozen observations, if not more. See if you can find things that most people, unless they were really paying attention, might not notice.

The When

The "when" of your setting is as important as the "where." You have several decisions to make.

What year is it? Is it a specific year like 1959, or just "the present"? Your choice of year will dictate everything from what sort of clothes the characters wear to more important issues like what is going on in the world and what are the attitudes of society at that time. For example, a play about a man of color dating a white woman in 1960 has a very different significance than it would if it were set in 2005.

What date or time of year is it? Buffalo, New York in the middle of January is an altogether colder and harsher place than it is in June. A play set on Christmas Day would create all kinds of special circumstances around it (e.g. stores closing early or already being closed, family gatherings, etc.), just as July 4th (in the United States) would (e.g. a parade, cookouts, fireworks).

What time of day is it? A twelve year old girl leaving her house at four in the afternoon is pretty common. She might be going to visit a friend or to dance lessons or a sports practice. Maybe she's waiting for a ride: if this were a movie, a minivan filled with other giggling twelve year old girls might be pulling up at any minute. But if she's slipping out her window at four in the morning…

Get ready for an exercise that will help you work on your "when."

EXERCISE: Choosing the "When"

Just like with our where exercise, given an action or a situation, decide what "when" would create the most tension. Keep in mind that your "when" might require a date, a time of year or a time of day—or it might best be described relative to another event. For example, if the situation was "a cowboy gets food poisoning," you might select to set your play "moments before the start of the rodeo steer-roping competition in which he's entered."

1. A student stealing the teacher's answer key.
2. A young person leaving for army boot camp.
3. A woman deciding not to get married.
4. An actor who gets stage fright.
5. A cook who has just burned dinner.

Changing the "When": Multiple Scenes

Ten-minute and one-act plays usually happen in one continuous period. The play begins at a certain time and runs until it ends, with no jumps or breaks in time (or place). But in some one-acts there are multiple scenes, and in longer plays, there may not only be multiple scenes but multiple acts. For instance, the first scene in the play takes place on a Friday night, and the second scene occurs the following morning. There is, therefore, a gap between the two scenes. When this happens, ask yourself the same questions about the second scene that you did for the first: what choice of "when" will create the most tension?

Just as in the case of the where, your goal with the when—no matter how many scenes you have—is to choose moments that heighten the conflict and tension. With each new when, we should be that much closer to the boiling point.

Chapter 4

STRUCTURING YOUR PLAY

Play Structure the Easy Way

Playwright and dramaturg Leon Katz once described the two essential elements of play structure. He said that in the beginning, what's going on should make the audience say, "that's interesting" and keep watching. By the end, "that's interesting" should turn to "wow."

While there are many ways (see **Alternate Play Structures** next) to structure your play, we're going to focus on an oldie but a goodie: three-act structure.

Think of a play as having three parts. Let's call them—big surprise— the beginning, middle and end. And a crucial part of that beginning, middle and end are our characters and conflict. Here's how it works:

We'll start with two characters, Jack and Jill. In the beginning of the play, we introduce the conflict. Jack wants Jill's pail of water. Jill says no. Conflict.

If Jack says, "OK. Fine. Have a nice day, Jill," the play is over. So he can't do this. Instead, there must be some really good reason why Jack can't walk away. Maybe he's dying of thirst. Jill has the only water for miles, and if Jack doesn't get water in the next ten minutes, he's going to die. There is now something at stake for Jack. If he doesn't get the water, he'll die. And not only that, there's a "ticking time bomb," so the play has a sense of urgency. For Jack, it's not just a want: it's a need. All of this can be set up in the beginning.

As we move to the middle of the play, Jack tries different tactics. Maybe he tries to bribe Jill with money or a goldfish or a new Porsche. Maybe he threatens to beat her up. But Jill needs the water too. She needs it to wash her dog before it competes in a dog show, and her family needs the prize money or they'll starve to death. Whatever the reason, it has to be good. Remember, Jack is running out of time. Things are getting desperate.

That leaves the end. One of four things can happen. One, Jack gets what he wants. He takes the pail from Jill and drains it on the spot. Jack is saved for now, but Jill is without water to wash the dog, and it's curtains for her and her family. Two, Jill gets what she wants. Jack may drop dead, but the dog wins the show and Jill's family gets the prize money. Three, they both get what they want. Jack drinks just enough to get to the next water hole, and Jill has some water left—the dog gets second place, which still nets her family enough prize money to survive a little longer. Not as much as before, but enough to get by. (This one is unlikely, because if you set it up right, nothing but total victory will give the characters what they need.) Four, neither gets what they want. They fight over the pail, spill the water, and everybody's doomed. No matter what the play, these possibilities are always the same—only the names and details change.

That's it, folks. A beginning introduces the characters, the conflict, the stakes and a ticking time bomb. The middle escalates the conflict and develops the characters as they change tactics. In the end, they either get it or they don't.

The problem with three-act structure is that at some point—mostly in screenwriting—people started looking at it as carved in stone. It's not. There are no page numbers on which certain events need to happen, as some screenwriting teachers would have you believe. As long as you follow the basic principle of characters needing something really badly and constantly working to get that thing, you'll be just fine.

Alternate Play Structures

If you're just starting out, it's best to stick to the three-act structure, which works perfectly well and is still the most used structure around. But not every play (and not every story you want to tell) works best with that structure, or at least with that structure alone. You'll be happy to know that there are other storytelling options out there, options that can complement and enhance an otherwise "traditional" play structure, or even stand on their own as a new structure entirely. Once again, if you're starting out, I strongly suggest that you skip this section and come back to it later in your writing development. But if you're still reading...

We begin with the landscape play. Landscape plays are simple to explain, though not nearly so easy to write well. They begin with very little information about where we are or the given circumstances of the play (e.g. the setting and the characters), almost as if they're an artist's blank canvas. But as the play continues, it fills in more and more of the landscape. An example of such a play is Beckett's *Endgame*, in which only gradually does the world of the play, its landscape, get painted for us.

A form of the landscape structure uses a technique called gapping, or gapped structure. In this structure, your play consists of a series of scenes. Between each scene, time has passed (i.e. a gap). For example, Scene One takes place in April, and Scene Two is in May. A gap can be an hour or a day, or it can be a decade. In *The Long Christmas Dinner* by Thornton Wilder, the entire play takes place at the Christmas dinner table, but it stretches over a period of years. Another type of gapped play has all of its major events (e.g. a murder, a wedding, an auto accident, etc.) happen during the gaps. What keeps the audience engaged by gapped plays is not so much what happens during the scenes (though they of course need to be interesting), but what happens between them. After each gap, the audience has to catch up and figure out what happened while they weren't watching; you're making them play detective as they fill in the landscape of your play.

In anecdotal structure, the play is made up of a series of characters seemingly going along on their own separate stories. But by the end of the play, the stories have all intersected into one. Imagine five different threads, none of them touching, but as you move closer to one end, the threads get closer and closer until they knot. A perfect example is Tony Kushner's *Angels in America*, in which Hannah Pitt becomes a mother figure to Prior, whose story seemed completely separate earlier in the play—and this is just one of many stories that intersect. In the film world, *Crash* recently made use of this same structure, with the stories of seemingly unconnected characters all crashing into one another.

Another structure is that of the process play. This sort of play is structured around some particular event, some particular process. For example, two women are having dinner. When dinner ends, so does the play. *Fences* by August Wilson has a strong process element, with Troy Maxson building a fence throughout the play—once he finishes, the play wraps up. A similar example from the film world (and also one involving building) is *Life as a House*, in which the event of the film is Kevin Kline's character building his dream home. Once the home is complete, the movie ends.

The last structural alternative I'll discuss here is the non-linear play. In most plays, the events happen in order. First comes Sunday, then Monday, then Tuesday. But not every play is like that. In *Betrayal* by Harold Pinter, for example, each scene we watch happens before the one we just saw. In other words, we begin at the end of the characters' story and each successive scene moves us closer to the beginning of that story (in this case, when two of the characters met, many years before). Why do that? The plot in *Betrayal* is one we've heard many times before: a couple meets, marries and then eventually breaks up because of marital infidelity. But by reversing the chronology, Pinter takes the focus off of what happens, which isn't all that interesting, and instead puts it on who these people are and how they got to the point at which the play begins, which is fascinating. It's like watching the unpeeling of an onion, with each new layer helping us understand the characters and their motives a little better.

Another example of non-linear structure is Tom Stoppard's *Arcadia*, which alternates between scenes set in the 1800s and scenes set in the present (in the same house), with an ending that brilliantly combines the two: the action in both time periods takes place simultaneously (though independently of each other). Still other plays might jump back and forth between any number of different time settings, or be mostly linear except for certain moments that take place out of the regular flow of time—or even out of "real" time. There is no rule that says that time must flow "normally," but since time is usually what gives order to the events in a play, if time doesn't do it, you'll need to come up with something else that will.

There are many, many other alternate structures out there, and others wait to be discovered should necessity call them into being. Make sure you have a firm handle on the more traditional three-act structure, but if you feel that it doesn't serve your storytelling needs (or not entirely), there is nothing wrong with looking for alternatives.

The Question of the Play

We've talked about three-act structure, and we've talked about alternative organizing principles for your work. No matter what structure you use, I like to think about plays in terms of a dramatic question. I'm not talking about thematic questions, as in "what big questions does the play wrestle with?" Instead, I'm talking about the most basic question of all: what question is the audience waiting to have answered? What's keeping their butts in the seats? In *Hamlet*, it's "will Hamlet get revenge?" In Beckett's *Waiting for Godot*, it's "will Godot show up?"

Why does having a dramatic question help? Because it engages the audience. You're giving them a puzzle to put together, a sentence to complete, and they will work to do just that. It doesn't prevent them from being entertained while they're working. Take the example of the "whodunit." It's unquestionably among the most popular and entertaining types of plays around, and yet it has a dramatic question built-in by definition: the whole point is to figure out "whodunit."

Both the play's characters and its audience race to unravel the mystery.

Whether your play is a mystery, a comedy, something more serious (what people usually call "a drama") or any other genre, giving the audience a dramatic question to answer is the way to keep them with you.

To Outline or Not to Outline, That is the Question...

And it's a good question. Every writer is different. Of course, everyone's idea of an outline is different, too.

In history class, an outline for your term paper might be filled with Roman numerals, capital and lower case letters, numbers—you know the drill. Play outlines rarely look like that. Instead, they're more likely to consist of a series of events, one after the other. In screenwriting, some writers put each scene on a separate index card, which is pretty much the same thing. It just allows you to move the scenes around in an easy, visual way (of course, screenplays have many more scenes).

Why outline? Outlining works. An outline forces you to think about your play (and especially the plot of your play), and it keeps you from going off on a tangent that ends up having to be thrown out later.

Personally, I do a limited amount of outlining before I begin, making sure I have a grasp of the major events of the play, and that I understand my characters and what they want. I might make a few major notes for each scene (in screenwriting, because of the number of scenes, I outline thoroughly). But I also view my outline as a work-in-progress, not something carved in stone. In other words, when the actual writing begins, if the play feels right going in a different direction than my outline, that's where it goes. At least in my first draft, I listen to my characters, not my notes.

The danger of outlining too much, particularly if you don't feel free to change when you write your play, is that it can drain the imagination and the life right out of your writing. It suddenly becomes "paint by numbers," where you're mechanically filling in what you have planned—and that's no fun.

So outline away, but remember that an outline is just a starting place and that your finished play, if you think of a play as a family member, may be less like the outline's twin and more like its distant cousin.

The One-Liner and the Synopsis

Whether or not you decide to do a full outline, other options to consider are the one-liner and the synopsis.

A one-liner is exactly what it sounds like—well, almost. It's not necessarily one line, but it should be just one sentence, and that one sentence should give us the main action of the play and the characters involved. Why is it important to have a one-liner? Do you need one before you start writing?

In Hollywood, agents often ask, "what's the one-liner on your script?" Of course, they're talking about screenplays, and they want a one-liner to see if they want to read your script in the first place—to see if it sounds like something they can sell. Wait a second, you're thinking—aren't we talking about plays? Yes, we are. And we haven't even written our scripts yet, so it's a little early to think about pitching them to agents.

But the reason we still talk about a one-liner—and why a one-liner is so important—is because if you can't describe what your play is about in a sentence, chances are you don't know enough about the story to write it. In other words, the one-liner is the ultimate organizing tool.

For example, in my comic one-act *The White Pages*, the one-liner is "A customer takes matters into his own hands when he discovers a used bookstore is removing the pages from classic books and replacing them with blank ones." One sentence tells us that the play is set in a used bookstore, that this particular bookstore is doing something to the books, and that a customer stands up to them in some way. We have the setting, the main character and the main action/conflict. We've completely organized our play, but there's still plenty of room for creativity.

A synopsis is an expanded one-liner. Often, during the submission process, theatres may ask for a one-page (maximum) synopsis, but while we're still in the construction process, don't worry about length; the synopsis can be as long as it needs to be. What exactly is it? Think of it as an outline, but written in short story form. At its most basic level, a synopsis describes what happens in each "act" (assuming a three-act structure) of your play. Or to explain it even more simply, it's a summary of the play's major events. Some writers like to go scene-by-scene, while others do more of a general synopsis. It's up to you. The bottom line is that the outline, the one-liner and the synopsis are all tools to help you organize your thoughts without feeling boxed in.

Sample Synopsis

This is from my musical, *Day One*. Synopses for plays and musicals are the same, though in musicals, writers will often mention song titles if they have them. Notice how the character names are in CAPS the first time we meet them—this is just to alert the reader that a new character has entered the story. This synopsis is a detailed one, but your synopsis could just be a paragraph or two, particularly if it's a shorter play.

It's the morning of the first day of school. All over the stage, characters sing about their hopes and fears for the year. For JAKE and STANLEY, seniors and best friends, it's about the excitement of finally being on top. STELLA, a senior transfer, wants to make friends. ERIKA, junior class president, wants to become student council president, while SKEETER, a freshman boy, just wants to avoid getting stuffed into his locker. And BLAISE, a senior, hates the school and everyone in it; she wants to get the year over with.

Stella, not knowing anyone, falls in with the "aspiring" crowd. Stanley, who's been looking for a Stella for the longest time, drafts her into his and Jake's circle. The year is shaping up to be a great one, and the three of them make a pact to make it last forever as they sing "This Place This Time."

But while they want the year to last forever, for Skeeter, it can't be over soon enough, and he sings how he wants out in "Muhammad Ali." Erika, wanting a toadie, suggests that he stick with her and she'll get him through during "The Solution is Clear." She hates this year too. If only there were a way to get it over with. And they're not the only ones: Blaise, as anti-social as they come and rumored to be dangerous, wants high school to be over just as badly.

The mysterious THYME arrives, and as she sings "Fifteen Minutes," time seems to move backward. Jake, Stanley and Stella take note, though they're not sure what has happened.

At lunch, a RAGGED FRESHMAN staggers into the cafeteria. Something awful has happened in the library: an explosion. Enter HELEN, Jake's old flame, back from her mysterious disappearance amid rumors that she's been practicing voodoo. As she sings "Melt Into Me," Jake seems ready to pick up where he left off—worshipping her.

Blaise is interested in Jake, but she decides that it could never happen in "Out Past Infinity."

Helen leads Jake, Stanley and Stella in magic rites to try to slow time. They capture Skeeter to be their sacrifice as they sing "Don't Let it Splatter." Meanwhile, Erika leads her followers, the WANNABES, in a rally for underclass rights. Blaise is caught between the two groups, wanting time to move forward, but unable to stop being interested in Jake. As Act I ends, Helen is on the verge of sacrificing Skeeter (apparently for real), while the Wannabes, in the middle of their rally, compete with Helen's magic.

As Act Two opens, Jake and the other seniors talk Helen out of sacrificing Skeeter. The scene becomes the locker room, where Skeeter is trying to get dressed before the seniors come in. He sings "Locker Room Blues" before the scene melts into the "Year Long

Limbo"—Skeeter and the rest of the cast limbo through the entire school year, amidst talk of a handsome Swedish exchange student, the Wannabes' great hope, whose arrival is always getting delayed. By the end of the limbo, it's the last day of school.

Still no exchange student, but Erika and the Wannabes are nearly there and liking their chances as they sing "New School Order." The final dance of the year is that night, and it's tradition that the seniors hand over the senior gavel just before the last dance of the evening.

Jake and company grow desperate; their high school years are almost over. Helen suggests that they kidnap Thyme to stop the clock: "If Thyme can't move, then time can't move." As they sing "Lost Sheep," Jake and Stanley let themselves be persuaded to help Helen, but Stella won't, and she and Stanley have a fight. Stella runs off.

Jake and Stanley kidnap Thyme, securing her in an abandoned janitor's closet, while Helen finds Stella and tells her that she can do better than Stanley, encouraging Stella to sing "I Hate Stanley" after Helen exits.

Meanwhile, a captive Thyme, alone with Jake, goes to work on him, playing on his doubts in "Sand." Jake flees, running into the Wannabes, who are eager to reel him in, singing "Come on, Jake." But just as Jake seems lost, Blaise appears, scaring off the Wannabes and declaring her love for him in "Sturdy and Strong." Helen walks in on them and becomes furious that she's lost Jake, but no amount of threat and persuasion can break up Jake and Blaise.

Helen, after another of a series of run-ins (literally) with Skeeter, finds Stanley, where she embellishes Stella's anger at Stanley and attempts to win Stanley for herself in "I Hate Stanley" (reprise). Stanley wavers, but in the end, fights Helen's magic—he loves Stella too much. Stanley seeks out Stella, and "In a Heartbeat" begs for forgiveness. But it's not enough for Stella, who leaves Stanley on his knees.

Jake and Blaise return to find Stanley laid low, and help him realize that he needs to stop trying to be Brando's Stanley Kowalski.

Stanley—whose real name is Hugo—rushes off to get ready for the dance, as Jake decides that he has to let Thyme go, even if it means that the year will end.

Jake convinces Stella, Stanley and Helen to join him and Blaise right before the dance—all are there to release Thyme. Stella reconciles with Stanley/Hugo, and all proceed to the dance, where Helen, left with no partner, ends up with the now-spunky Skeeter. The SWEDISH EXCHANGE STUDENT finally arrives, but to the enormous disappointment of the Wannabes, it's a girl. As the cast dances and sings the "Finale," Jake hands over the senior gavel to Erika, and all prepare to move on to the new challenges and day ones that await them.

EXERCISE: Incubate Your One-Liners

Given each of the following one-liners, help them grow into a short paragraph synopsis of your play, creating whatever new details you need. If you're doing this in a classroom situation, how do your synopses compare to the ones your classmates came up with? Notice, by the way, that the third one-liner is in the form of a question.

1. When a teenage girl discovers that her parents are shipping her off to boarding school, she sets out to get her sentence commuted.

2. A Little League pitcher refuses to take the mound, wiling to risk forfeiting the game to stand up for a friend.

3. When the school board won't let a drama teacher stage a play, what will she do to give her students what she feels they desperately need?

Decisions, Decisions

As we get ready to write, more decisions loom ahead. How long should my play be? When someone asks me this, my response is usually "as long as it needs to be." On the one hand, it's a truthful answer, but I can understand that you may not think it's a helpful one. It can be dangerous to try to squeeze a story into a predetermined length, but I also understand that sometimes you may have an assignment or the particular contest you're entering requires work of a certain length.

As you consider the question of length, remember that ten-minute plays generally have one main idea and conflict, and the play is pretty much just about that; there's not time for anything else. One-act plays, which are the next step up in length, usually run up to an hour, though that's long for a one-act (considering they often play in festivals and competitions with other pieces). Technically, there's no limit to the length of a one-act: the name just means that there is one act. But usually they have one location and very few (maybe only one) scenes. Since one-acts tend to appear on bills with other one-acts, they need to have a set that can be changed relatively easily: you're not the only one who will have to use the stage that day. Full-length plays are so named because they fill up a bill on their own. They tend to run at least 70-80 minutes, but be careful with anything over 2 hours; if we're going to sit in a theater for that long, it had better be great.

One final thing to remember before we leave the issue of length is that not all ideas are created equal. Not every idea will support a full-length play, or even a long one-act. For example, I have a ten-minute play, *Menagerie*, about a strained romance on Valentine's Day. It's a clever little play and a lot of fun for ten minutes, but as currently conceived, it shouldn't be anything longer than a ten-minute play. There's just not enough to it. That doesn't make it inferior. It just means that its length is right as it is. Could I turn it into a full-length play? Sure, but the idea would have to undergo much more development, and ultimately it would be a very different piece.

Another decision is whether you're writing a comedy or a more serious play (drama isn't really the opposite of comedy, though many people use it that way). The running joke about the plays of Shakespeare is that the way to tell the comedies from the tragedies (the true opposite of comedy) is that in the former, everybody gets married, while in the latter, everybody dies. Personally, I rarely decide that "this time I'm writing a comedy." I know what I want to write about, and the play comes out a certain way, because that's how I write.

But what if it's a serious subject? Surely that means the play has to be serious. Actually, when I wrote *Now You See Me*, I did the opposite. Why? Serious subjects treated with non-stop seriousness are tough for audiences to take; it's like someone grating their nails against a chalkboard for an entire class period. Everyone needs a break. And in making an audience laugh, you relax them and open them up, making them more likely to be receptive to your play and what it has to say or to show them. In fact, think of the power of a play that has kept an audience laughing all the way through—and it's only at the end that the urgency and seriousness of the situation hits them. How much more powerful will that realization be if they don't see it coming?

On a final comedic note, whether the subject of your play is serious or not, if you decide to write comedy, remember that humor usually comes out of the situations in which the characters find themselves, not from clever wordplay or inside jokes. Inside jokes may work well at your school or with the few people who know them, but since most of us aren't in on the joke, we won't find them funny and will probably be confused.

For what audience are you writing? If the play is going to be put on at your school (or for any "all ages" audience), that may place some restrictions on your content (e.g. profanity and adult situations). And remember, as I noted earlier, schools tend to like larger casts with more women than men. If you know you're writing for that market, it's not wise to write a play that's small-cast, mostly male or full of four-letter words.

Ultimately, no matter what practical choices you make, telling a great story is the crucial ingredient. But exercising some common sense can go a long way in making sure that great story finds a receptive market.

Chapter 5

WRITING DIALOGUE

Dialogue Basics

Dialogue is what the characters say. Their words. Dialogue is usually directed at another character on the stage, though occasionally a character will say something to the audience, to himself or even to another character who isn't there at the moment. (Monologues are a special category of dialogue, but more on them later.)

Why do we need dialogue in a play? Because in theatre, the dialogue, along with the characters' behavior (what they do), is what tells the story. Yes, it's possible to write a play without dialogue (in other words, the characters don't speak and we have to rely on their actions and things like sound and set and lights to tell the story), but the overwhelming majority of plays depend on it. Not only does good dialogue advance the story/plot/conflict, but it also helps develop the character speaking it, both by what the character says and how she says it.

Want to write great dialogue? Before you can learn how to make characters talk in ways that people remember, you have to learn to listen.

EXERCISE: Listen!

The next time you're with your friends at lunch, take a few minutes to listen—without talking. Listen for how many times they don't finish their sentences. Listen for "filler words" (examples are "well," "like" and "um"). Listen for how many times they repeat themselves, and think about how much of what you hear moves the conversation forward and how much just goes in circles. Try making a mental tally each time you learn a new piece of information. Speaking of information, it's time to talk about...

Exposition

Exposition is another word for information. In a play, exposition is the setting up of the story and the characters in it. It has to be done, of course, and dialogue is a major tool for doing it. Characters talk, and we learn things. Seems easy enough, but handling exposition can be a thorn in the side of even experienced writers. What do we need to know about the characters and their situations? When do we need to know it? Give an audience too much too soon, and there's nothing to learn later: they'll be bored. On the other hand, if you don't tell them enough, they'll be confused.

Jose Rivera (author of *Marisol* and creator of the TV show *Eerie, Indiana*) once likened the flow of exposition to an IV drip, and suggested that one should only give enough to keep the body alive. It's a great analogy.

There used to be a convention in plays some time ago in which we overheard the maid talking on the telephone. In this conversation, which typically began the play, all of the given circumstances would be explained to the audience. Today, we find that laughable, as evidenced by Tom Stoppard's hilarious send-up of the convention in *The Real Inspector Hound*, when Mrs. Drudge, on the phone, answers the caller by saying, "I'm afraid there is no one of that name here, this is all very mysterious and I'm sure it's leading up to something. I hope nothing is amiss for we, that is Lady Muldoon and her houseguests, are here cut off from the world, including Magnus, the wheelchair-ridden half-brother of her ladyship's husband Lord Albert Muldoon who ten years ago went out for a walk on the cliffs and was never seen again…" You'd never be that obvious—right? If you're not careful, sometimes you can be without even realizing it.

One way to protect from exposition overload is to avoid having characters volunteer information. Instead, have it pulled out of them by another character, or have a character use it as a tactic to get what he wants. For example, having Judy tell Mark that she just got married can merely be a boring fact. But if Mark is in the middle of begging Judy to take him back and Judy tells him she just got married, now it's a revelation.

"Show, don't tell," is one of the most important commandments in playwriting (and indeed in all dramatic writing). Anything that a character can do rather than say, let the character do. For example, Jane doesn't need to say "I'm afraid" if she can hide under a bed.

And remember, what a character does NOT say can be just as important as what he does. This forces the audience to fill in the blanks. (Stay tuned for Jeff Sweet's fantastic **Unspoken Word** exercise coming up shortly.) And always…

Beware the Exposition Enabler

Two brothers, Ross and Floss, sit on a bench.

ROSS
I can't believe Mr. Smith really left his wife.

FLOSS
Yeah. Did he say where he was going?

ROSS
Roswell, New Mexico.

FLOSS

What's he doing there?

ROSS

What does anybody do in Roswell? Wait for the aliens, of course.

It's purposely written to be a terrible scene. There's no conflict or dramatic action of any kind. The scene exists only to give us information. Floss is what I call an "exposition enabler," because he contributes nothing to the scene on his own: the only reason he's there is to allow Ross to tell us about the Smiths.

When a character shows up in a scene (and certainly in a play as a whole), it should be for a reason. That reason may be to fulfill a certain function (e.g. teacher, messenger, guard, salesperson, etc), but it can't be just to help another character tell us things.

EXERCISE: The Unspoken Word

I learned this exercise from my friend, accomplished playwright Jeff Sweet, and it's a great one. Here's how it works: come up with two characters talking about some issue that is causing tension between them. For example, maybe the first character has lost the second character's homework. Your job is to write a short conversation (approximately a page) between the two characters, but to take the trigger word in this conversation (in this case, it might be "lost") and leave it out. In other words, no matter how the characters talk around it, the word "lost" will never be used. This creates extra tension, because there's this unspoken word, the proverbial "elephant in the room," that nobody is mentioning.

Here's an example of how such a conversation (this one is not about homework) might begin:

MICHAEL

You can barely see it.

EXERCISE: The Unspoken Word (cont'd)

MICHAEL'S DAD

Barely see it? It's the size of a yardstick.

MICHAEL

It's no big deal. I can paint over it.

MICHAEL'S DAD

You can't paint over it without painting everything. How could you let this happen?

MICHAEL

The other guy parked too close. It's not my fault he tried to park an SUV where it says "compact cars only."

This conversation could go on endlessly. What was the unspoken word? If you guessed "scratch," you were right. Now see what you can do with your own unspoken word.

Keep It in Context

When I was in high school, I was editor of the school newspaper, *Mar News*. The Mar Newsies, as we were called—we had our own room, a shared history, our own style of speech and words that only had meaning to us. For those who opened the door and looked in, I'm sure they had no idea what we were talking about and thought we were weirdos or Martians or worse. But to us, all of this was perfectly normal: if someone brought up the band PIGG, for example, we would have known that, of course, they were referring to the fictitious band with the legendary anthem "To Umpbumpulon." Of course.

Groups of people who know each other are like that. If you work with someone or live with someone or see someone regularly, you know things about each other. Maybe like the Mar Newsies, you've invented your own ways of communicating. In any case, you don't have to spend the first five minutes of every conversation introducing yourselves or explaining what you do, because certain facts are already known and understood. Your dialogue is what we call high-context.

For example, here's a brief conversation between a mother and her daughter.

MOM
Did you get it?

DAUGHTER
No. They were out.

MOM
I told you not to wait until the last minute.

Even without going any further, just from what they say (forget that they're "Mom" and "Daughter") it's clear that the two characters have a history with each other. The object ("it") doesn't need to be identified more at this point; both of them know what it is.

But what if the same conversation were between the daughter and a complete stranger? It would be very different.

STRANGER
That dress in the store window was lovely.

DAUGHTER
They didn't have any in my size.

STRANGER
I hope you didn't need it right away.

In this second conversation, the characters have to provide much more information, as they don't know each other; there is no shared history or language between them. We call their dialogue low-context.

Levels of Dialogue

I'd like to share a wonderful lesson about "levels" of dialogue from my old mentor, Leon Katz.

Leon used to talk about dialogue as having three (at least) levels. First-level dialogue would be something like a school principal telling a student, "If you don't tell me who else vandalized the math room, you're suspended from school." It's right there on the surface, no mystery at all. Next is second-level dialogue: "If I don't find out who vandalized the math room, someone's going to get suspended." The principal is still saying "tell me or else," but it's more indirect, leaving the audience to "complete the sentence." Third-level dialogue is the most indirect of all. In that same situation, it might begin with the principal saying, "I remember five years ago when someone stole all of the English textbooks. No one would confess to it"—and then launch into a story about how a group of students were eventually caught and served lengthy suspensions that kept them out of the colleges of their choice. The character (and the audience) hears the story and makes the connection; it has the same meaning as the first-level dialogue, but it's a more interesting way of saying it.

While indirect dialogue (in other words, second and third-level dialogue) is laden with subtext (literally, subtext is the meaning "below the text"—what is really meant by the words) and potentially engages the audience to a much greater degree by forcing them to figure out its riddle, you should never rely on ANY of these levels of dialogue exclusively. Direct dialogue has its place too, particularly when characters are angry. So best to mix 'em up!

Punctuation Power

Punctuation. The mere mention of the word strikes fear in the hearts of most students. After all, how many times have you gotten back a paper only to find that it looks like someone bled to death on it? Believe it or not, at least in playwriting, punctuation is your friend.

Punctuation is a big part of how we create rhythm in our plays. In fact, punctuating your play carefully is the best way to make your intentions clear to the director and the actors—so think carefully about what punctuation you use. What are your choices?

. (the period) means a complete break at the end of a sentence.
I want you to leave. I want you to leave now.

? (the question mark) is, as you might imagine, for questions.
Why are you leaving?

Note: Some playwrights (including yours truly) occasionally like to use periods at the end of sentences that naturally seem to require a question mark. It's a way to tell an actor that you're looking for a specific type of delivery.

MR. A

I can't seem to find my dog.

MRS. B

Your dog.

MR. A

Yes. My dog.

As you can see, *your dog* is caught somewhere between being a question and being a statement. What's the difference? For one thing, we tend to sound a little different when we ask a question as opposed to when we make a statement. Try saying, for example, "I go to school here" and "do I go to school here?" aloud. Now compare how your voice sounds. From a writing standpoint, the difference is that characters who make statements sound more in control than ones who ask questions. In the conversation above, Mrs. B's question, because it sounds more like a statement, makes her stronger than if she just asked, "Your dog?"

, (the comma) is like a bridge or a slide from one part of a sentence to another. It's a much shorter rest than a period, a sort of half-breath.
I want you to leave now, and I want you to leave the new dress I bought you.

! (the exclamation point) is a period that got excited. Use it for extra emphasis, or when a character is shouting (you can add ALL CAPS or even use italics if you really want to emphasize the shouted text).
Stop! It's a trap!
Beware of overusing the exclamation point, though, or it loses its power.

— (the em dash) is a hitch in a sentence. It's almost like in music, where there's a moment of syncopation.
I want you to leave—and leave the new dress I bought you.
An em dash is also the way to show that one character is interrupting another one.

MS. A
I want to—

MR. B
Be quiet.

; and : (semicolon and colon) are less commonly used in dialogue. The semicolon connects two related sentences—usually where the second sentence follows from the first—and thus it falls close to a period in the length of the break it makes (think a period, with just a dash of comma in it). The colon sets off a list of items or emphasizes a comment or explanation that will follow it. It's similar in feel to a semicolon, perhaps just a notch closer to a period in the length of the break it creates.
I'm going with you; it's the fastest way for me to get home.
Here are the things I need: thyme, rosemary, parsley and sage.

… (ellipses) are for when a character either trails off at the end of a sentence, or pauses to think of his next word in the middle of a sentence.
I can't find the . . .

Something seems to be . . . missing.

How do you know what mark of punctuation to choose, or whether the one you picked is the right one? Try having someone else (or possibly several other people) read your sentences out loud. That way, you know if the actors are interpreting the rhythm of your words how you want. If not, time to adjust your punctuation.

EXERCISE: The Many Faces of Punctuation

Depending on your punctuation choice, each simple sentence below can take on a totally different rhythm and feel. I'm not just talking about the end of the sentences—try changing the punctuation in the middle too. See what you come up with!

1. Here we go again
2. I'm babysitting your puppy
3. She's running away from home
4. This is so meaningful
5. I told you not to leave me

More Dialogue Tips

On stage, we have a limited amount of time. We don't have time for filler words like "well" or long conversations about the weather. We have to edit.

Real people often use contractions when they speak. Is your character the type of person who would use them, or not?

Be consistent. A guy who can't put a grammatical sentence together one minute shouldn't sound like an English professor the next minute. Make sure that the words a character uses are consistent with his education and background.

Different people are different people to different people. You don't talk to your parents the same way you talk to your friends. You may not even use the same words. (Yes, it sounds like a total contradiction of the last tip, but it's really not.)

Try imagining a particular actor you know (or even a famous one) in the role. Often, when you can visualize your character very specifically, it's easier to make her talk. It doesn't matter that the actor will probably never do the role.

Characters don't generally speak in a "your turn, my turn" kind of way. They want what they want, and they want it now. Their dialogue needs to be infused with that want—it makes them want to talk, rather than patiently let other characters make long speeches.

Vary your rhythms. Don't have every character's lines be the same length or have the same punctuation all of the time. Short, staccato passages can serve as a great counterpoint to longer lines, helping keep your audience more engaged. If everything sounds the same, your audience may fall asleep! Here is a passage from *Beef Junkies*:

COWGIRL
(shaking)

Where's the cow?

SHEPHERD

What's wrong with *her*?

COWBOY

She's dead.

SHEPHERD

She just talked.

COWBOY

That wasn't talking. That was shaking.

SHEPHERD

I thought I heard "where's the cow?"

COWBOY

Teeth chattering probably. Tongue gets into the act, and you never know what might come out. It's all involuntary muscle reflexes. I once saw a dead man stand up, recite the Gettysburg Address backward and then choke the man standing next to him. They had to pry his ice cold hands off the man's throat.

(beat)

Dead people can do extraordinary things. Don't sell them short.

In this short exchange, about a half page of manuscript, there's a little bit of everything: sentence fragments, very short statements and equally short questions (as short as two or three words), more complex sentences, a rest (i.e. "beat") and even a mini-monologue. While every moment of your play can't be filled with this kind of diversity, strive for as much variety as you reasonably can.

Monologues

A monologue is any speech by one character. While there's no ironclad rule that stipulates how long a character's speech needs to be to qualify as a monologue, a good rule of thumb is at least 30 seconds. There is no limit to how long a monologue can be, and there are even one-person plays, in which the entire piece is written to be performed by one actor (e.g. *Golda's Balcony*, *I Am My Own Wife* or my very own teen backyard wrestling play *Yard Wars*).

Monologues are usually part of a larger play, but sometimes they are written to stand alone (e.g. for forensics competitions, most likely). There may or may not be another character on stage. I tend to be cautious about having long monologues in my plays, because if you're not careful, a monologue can bring a play's forward motion to a grinding halt. Also, since people almost never talk that way in real life, if a play is meant to be "realistic," monologues will take away from that reality.

But a good monologue can be gold. It can be a much-needed change of pace, giving the audience a chance to catch its collective breath. And it allows a character to go to a completely different place, and to take us with her: one particularly memorable monologue is in *Long Day's Journey into Night* (Eugene O'Neill), when Mary Tyrone takes us out of her miserable present and back through the fog of her mind to a happier time when she had just met James Tyrone and fallen in love.

Actors love monologues, because it's a chance for them to shine, and from a practical standpoint, they need them for auditions. So if you want to write a monologue, whether as part of a play or as a stand-alone, remember a few tips:

- A monologue is like a mini-play or scene in that it has its own beginning, middle and end.

- The character delivering the monologue must want something in the present. In other words, why is he telling us this? What does he want right now, and how is delivering the monologue helping him get it? Monologues whose only purpose is to describe something that happened don't work.

- Like dialogue, monologues have two primary functions: to move the plot/story forward and to tell us more about the character. That doesn't mean that the character literally should tell us about herself. We should learn more about her from what she says and from how she says it.

- A helpful tip, if you have a character telling us a story about something that happened in the past, is to begin the monologue in the past tense and then switch to the present. For example, "When I was little, I went to the supermarket with my dad every chance I got. He'd say he was going shopping, and almost before he got the words out, I was in the car. Only I'm sitting in the front seat this time, my first time I don't have to sit in the back, and he lets me be in charge of the radio…" Using the present tense, even to describe something in the past, puts us right there with the character and helps energize your monologue.

EXERCISE: The Worst Birthday Party Ever Monologue

Create a character (briefly) who tells us about the worst birthday party
ever. Keep in the back of your mind that your character is telling
another character this to convince that second character not to have a
birthday party.

The Narrator: Friend or Foe?

Many young playwrights instinctively write a narrator into their plays.
I'm not sure who gave them this idea, but most of the time, it's a bad
one. Why? Because it's a cheat.   The idea of playwriting is that we
learn about the story and the characters and the conflict (in fact, about
everything) by watching what happens between the characters on the
stage.   Remember the playwriting mantra "show, don't tell"?
Narrators are the ultimate tell, a crutch for playwrights who aren't
confident in their own ability to show us the story on the stage.

That sounds so final. Can a narrator ever work? Of course. The
narrator—in this case the Stage Manager—works wonderfully in *Our
Town* by Thornton Wilder, and my friend Matt Buchanan uses a
narrator effectively in his plays *Prince Ugly* and *The Day Boy and the
Night Girl*. What makes these narrators work when so many others
don't?   The difference between an effective narrator and an
ineffective one is that the "good" narrator is more than just someone
who gives us information. He is a character in his own right, and
through telling the story, he develops a relationship either with the
other characters, with the audience or with both. It takes considerable
skill to pull this off, though, and most plays don't need it, so think
carefully before going the narrator route.

Using Profanity

For a play to sound "real," characters need to use profanity. Not true.
I don't have a personal problem with hearing four-letter words, but in

most cases, they're just filler and don't add anything to the content of the dialogue.

But what if I have a character—for example a gang member—who just seems like the kind of person who ought to use profanity? To be honest, even with characters that in "real life" probably would use their share of four-letter words, once we (the audience) realize that they're not using them in the play, we get used to it. Whatever the rules of your play's world, as long as you establish them early and stick with them, your audience will accept them. We won't give the lack of profanity another thought.

Of course, if you're writing for the school market (I'd include community theatres as well), profanity is rarely acceptable, so you have a practical reason to avoid it. Sometimes if I have a word or a phrase that I consider borderline in terms of appropriateness for some markets (i.e. if it's done at a college it would be fine, but at a high school might not be), I will include both the original line and a potentially less offensive alternative, allowing the production to choose.

Chapter 6

THE ART OF WRITING STAGE DIRECTIONS

Plays are meant to be seen on the stage, not on the page—right? Right, but before it makes it to the stage, your play must make it through a small army of readers. I've been one. Assuming you survive the readers (and the literary manager and the artistic director) and your play gets produced, then there is the director, the actors, the designers, etc. Each of them wants as clear a picture of your play as possible. While your story may be largely told through dialogue, do not underestimate the importance of stage directions.

Stage directions break down into three main types: description, action and character direction/line readings.

Description
Description is how you establish the setting of the play and its characters. Typically, a play begins with a description of the setting: the when and the where. Descriptions can vary greatly in style and length, from the intensely detailed work of O'Neill, who goes on for several pages at the start of *The Iceman Cometh*, to Beckett's legendary *Waiting for Godot*, whose entire opening description is "A country road. A tree." Sometimes this opening description is called the "at-rise description," because it describes what is on stage when the curtain rises. Not all theaters have curtains anymore, but we sometimes still use the term. (To see what an opening might look like, go to the *War of the Buttons* opening in Appendix A.)

The other kind of description is character description. You should describe each character in the body of the script (not just on the Cast of Characters page, because it's annoying to have to keep flipping back to the beginning of the script all the time) as we meet him. It doesn't need to be lengthy, but a name and age (and gender, if there's any doubt), with a short phrase or sentence that gives a thumbnail "sketch," will help your reader picture the character and get a quick sense of who this person is. Remember, if I'm a producer, I want to know whom I can cast in the role: I want to know the character's age, gender and type. For example, in my own play *Ben*, Holly is described as "thirtysomething, professional-looking and cell phone in hand"—just enough to give a sense of her without slowing down the read. We'll learn more about her as the play goes on.

One thing NOT to do when describing characters: don't tell us things about the character we couldn't possibly know unless we read the description, because the audience doesn't have access to that information. For example, instead of the description for Holly above, let's say I wrote, "thirtysomething and secretly longing for a son." The only way we could know that Holly is secretly longing for a son is if either she or some other character gives us this information (by dialogue or action). Sitting in a dark theater, we certainly won't be able to read the character description in the script.

Action
Action is either what the characters do, or things the audience experiences. Let's start with what the characters (i.e. the actors) do. For example, "Richard exits" is an action. So is "Wendy throws Peter's trophy out the window." In both cases, what the characters do brings about a change in the circumstances on stage. This is the most important kind of action, the kind that no director or actor can reasonably cross out.

There are two other types of action: blocking and business. Blocking is literally the movement of the characters on the stage, and most of the time, it's best left to the director and the actors to figure out. Why write "Fred moves stage left" if he could just as easily move right? If Fred moving left is crucial to the action (for example, if he moved right, he'd see the killer hiding behind the curtain), that's different.

But otherwise, avoid writing blocking—it marks you as an amateur trying to direct the play off the page. Business is what the characters do on stage, but it's generally not of a crucial nature. For example, "Rick and Tim play cards." Sure, it might be interesting, but if they were playing darts, would it really be all that different? This is not to say you can't write business, but try to make choices that help develop your characters and advance the action in some way; don't be arbitrary and don't overdo it. Your goal when writing action: when a director or actor reads your script, he pays attention to every line, because he knows that all of it is important. The opposite is also true: if your script is full of picky, unnecessary stage directions that describe things down to the last detail, the director and actors are likely to ignore them all, which means the important ones get ignored too.

As for things the audience experiences, examples include "a car alarm goes off" or "there's the sound of a drum" or "smoke issues from offstage" or "the sun rises." These are the kinds of things that your technical staff and designers will note, and they can be just as crucial to your play.

Character Direction
Character direction is sometimes called a parenthetical, or less flatteringly, a "wryly." It occurs in the middle of a character's dialogue, and in its most useful form, the character direction may clarify an action.

SUSAN
(as she exits)

Don't follow me.

In this case, "as she exits" is both an action and a way of informing the character's line of dialogue that follows.

But too many inexperienced writers use character stage directions to try to direct the play, and this is the no-no that drives directors and actors to cross out your stage directions, sometimes even your useful ones. This ill-advised abuse of the parenthetical is more commonly referred to as a line reading. (The "wryly" nickname came about because "wryly" was the specific line reading given—and it stuck.)

CHUCK
(enthusiastically)
This is so awesome!

What's wrong with the parenthetical "enthusiastically"? What's wrong is that you're telling the actor how to say the line. But it's my play, you're thinking. Isn't it important that the lines are said the way I intended them to be said? Yes, but let the director and the actors do their jobs. The reality is that if you write your dialogue well and punctuate it carefully, there's little need for line readings. In the example above, the content and punctuation of the line make its meaning perfectly obvious without "enthusiastically."

Is there ever a time when it's OK to use a line reading? Yes. If you have a line that, if not clarified, could be taken the wrong way (for example, if a character means the opposite of what she is saying), you may want to clarify it with a parenthetical. But these occasions are typically few and far between.

HARLEY
(lying)
I love you so much.

In the example above, without the parenthetical, we wouldn't know that Harley was lying; we need "lying." Here are more quick tips for stage directions:

- Keep your stage directions as compact as possible and use active verbs. In other words, instead of "Jennifer is brushing her teeth" at the opening of a play, "Jennifer brushes her teeth." Note also that characters don't "sit down." They sit.

- Never use the past tense. Don't write "Mark exited." It's "Mark exits." Always write stage directions with the idea that you're describing events as they happen.

- Avoid "overdescribing" a character: "five-foot-three, with red hair and green eyes and heavyset." Unless it's crucial to the play, you're wasting time on something that's irrelevant. What if there's a really great actress who's five-foot-five or has brown hair? You'll come off as an amateur. (Yes, Eugene O'Neill did it, but he was Eugene O'Neill.) It's more important to describe a character's general type (e.g. fiery or a go-getter or bookish).

- When you feel the urge to use a line reading, instead try putting in a "pause" or a "beat." A pause is exactly what it sounds like, though its length is best left to individual productions to decide. A beat is similar to a pause, and some people use them interchangeably. For me, a beat indicates that there's not just a silence, but that there's a shift in the direction of the conversation at the same time. A play is divided into beats, but we call the spaces between these sections beats. I know—it's confusing, and you're probably wondering why I'd suggest using a pause or a beat instead of a line reading. To me, it's a way of saying to the director and the actors, "This is a thoughtful moment, but I am trusting you to decide how to interpret it." They might actually come up with something that you haven't thought of, something that you like better than your original idea. Keep an open mind.

- There's nothing wrong with giving your stage directions a little spin, but don't write a novel. A professor of mine, when talking about screenwriting, told me never to clump more than six lines of description together. In playwriting it's OK to break that law (you pretty much have to, because of differences in formatting), but it's not a bad thing to keep the spirit of it in the back of your mind.

- Unlike dialogue, which often reflects a character's quirks of speech or regional dialect, stage directions should be grammatical.

Ultimately, remember that stage directions are written to be read. Make them well-written, succinct and clear.

Chapter 7

WRITING THE FIRST DRAFT

The Playwriting Process

So you've done all of this work—thought up characters who want things, created a world in which they live, come up with a rough idea of how your play may go. Now it's time to let your characters loose on each other and on the world and let them interact. Time to start writing!

Everyone has different work habits. Some writers work to music, while others need silence. Some get up early in the morning and work for a certain number of hours each day. Others write late at night. Others write only when they're moved to do so. Some write in front of their computers at home, while others may have offices where they go to work. Personally, I like to write in restaurants and cafes; I can concentrate on my work, while someone brings me things to eat and drink (and I don't have to clean up!). It's not a bad arrangement, if you're able to block out the bustle of those kinds of places.

One thing that might (or might not) surprise you is that I usually write longhand (as in with a pen and a legal pad) first and then type what I write into the computer. The process of transferring my writing from the pad to the computer is the first step of my rewriting process, but more on that later. Let's get back to that first draft.

A first draft isn't supposed to be perfect. Not even close. Don't worry—just get started and keep going! Worried that the play isn't following your outline? It's OK. As we discussed earlier, outlines are just guidelines; they're not meant to be set in stone.

I have a screenwriter friend (he was a producer for a TV news magazine show) who would typically get halfway through his screenplays—we're talking 50 pages in—and then start second-guessing himself and rewriting the first half of the script before he had written the rest of it. As a consequence, he rarely finished a screenplay.

Even if you're not completely happy with everything you're writing, the time to rewrite is not while you're still working on the first draft. Your mission is to get to the end, because the most important thing is finishing. Don't stop until you have safely typed "Blackout. End of play."

Then the real work begins…

Opening Your Play

In track, getting out of the starting blocks quickly is important to winning a sprint. Hitting a home run in the first inning of a baseball game gives your team momentum. It's just as important to have a strong opening for your play.

No one, of course, intends to write a weak opening. But what makes for a strong one? An opening that creates that same momentum as in sports is what does. Here are four possible ways to help gain that momentum.

1. Start your play as late in the story as possible. In fact, it's often been said that you should begin as late as possible, and end as early as possible. (More on ending as early as possible later.) That means not having your audience sit through endless exposition as you set up "the story so far." As we discussed in **Exposition** (Chapter 5), just give us what we need as we need it. That way, we keep moving forward.

2. Start your play right after some "event" has happened. That event could be anything: a teenage boy has shoplifted a baseball glove, someone's grandmother has won the lottery or an athlete on a scholarship has broken an ankle. Let the energy and consequences of this event carry over into what we see on stage.

3. Start your play with the characters in the middle of a physical action. For example, maybe a woman frantically searches a room for some missing object, or a boy throws his clothing into a suitcase. These actions give the characters forward motion, and the audience will want to know why they're doing what they're doing.

4. Have a great opening line of dialogue. One of my all-time favorites is Jerry's simple opening line from Albee's brilliant one-act *The Zoo Story*: "I've been to the zoo." When Peter doesn't notice, Jerry continues: "I said, I've been to the zoo. MISTER, I'VE BEEN TO THE ZOO!" After that, we're sure interested in what happened at the zoo.

This is a Play, not a Movie

Generally speaking, a big problem for inexperienced writers (especially young writers, who have grown up with the movies and TV even more so than previous generations) is not understanding that plays are not movies, and that some things we see in the movies don't work on stage. While there are always exceptions, here are some things that work much better in a movie (or on TV) than they do in a live play. I'd suggest you avoid them.

1. The narrator. In movies, there is often voiceover narration. The reason why it works is because the person doing the voiceover is a character, someone who is fully involved in the story. For the narrator to work on stage, as I discussed earlier, the same conditions need to exist: the narrator needs to be a participant in the play, someone who is a character and not just a provider of information. It's not easy to pull off and not something I recommend—but if it's really necessary, it can be done.

2. Chase scenes involving vehicles. The only way a chase scene will work at all is if it's highly stylized (in other words, purposefully made not to look real).

3.   Violence or combat that has to look completely real and believable.

4. Writing characters' specific facial expressions. In many venues, the actors are just too far away for their faces to be seen clearly, and unlike in film, there is no such thing as a close-up.

5. Phone calls. Phone calls put characters in a static position. Two characters on the phone just isn't the same as two of them together on the live stage.

6. Animals. There are no retakes if the dog decides to get interested in something other than your play, to say nothing of the production issues involved.

7. Explosions or elaborate special effects. No matter what you do, they're never going to look completely real, and the more real they do look, the more expensive and difficult they'll be. On the other hand, stylized special effects can certainly work. For example, when I directed *Lord of the Flies*, we created a raging fire with some lighting gels and a smoke machine. If I hadn't had the smoke machine, I would have done the fire with lighting alone. Once we established the convention that "this is fire," the audience accepted it. In fact, you're often better off not trying to be too realistic; if your effects are obviously stylized, the audience is less likely to be bothered than if the effects are almost real but don't quite cut it.

8. Rapid scene shifts. While it's not impossible to use suggested settings to move a character from the top of a building to a basement in the space of a few seconds, this is much more common in film, where the director can "cut" from one scene to another in a single frame. If you need an actor to be in two totally different places on stage very quickly, get a hold of a prop not currently in his possession or complete a costume change, you need to allow for time to do this—

and making the audience sit in silence in the dark is not a good choice.

To this list, I'd also add a strong warning about dreams and flashbacks. Most of the time, they're not necessary. Dreams are what some would call "cheesy," and in the case of flashbacks, they're usually just giving us exposition that we don't need.

This is not to say that there aren't fun, theatrical ways to use some of the elements listed above. For example, a key element of farce (a style of comedy using absurd humor and improbable situations) is that a play's characters go in and out of the set's requisite three doors— always in such a way as to be very funny. For example, a doctor trying to see two different patients at once may keep shuttling them in and out of different rooms so that they don't see one another. So in some ways, it may almost feel like a chase, but it's a chase made for the stage. Sometimes writers who have needed to show phone calls will have the two characters stand in separate pools of light on stage. The phone worked hilariously in *Angels in America* (Tony Kushner), because Roy Cohn was on the phone and at the same time interacting with a live character on the stage. People have even played animals. It can work, because it's clear that the actors are not animals: the audience suspends its disbelief and accepts the convention.

Not only that, but the stage has unique possibilities for the precise reason that it's not tied to the same standards of "reality" as film and TV. For example, actors can play more than one character, and the audience will accept the convention that they're different people (it's amazing what slight changes to costumes or hair styles can do). In fact, you can even have the actor do the transformation right in front of us, again reminding the audience that they're watching a play. In *War of the Buttons*, the clothing that Charlie and Hugo hang up in Hugo's "moving in" scene becomes the clothing that is the spoils of war in the next; a prop or set piece used for one purpose in one scene can turn into something entirely different right before our eyes, and if it's written well, it will be totally believable to the audience.

The bottom line is that just because something doesn't look "real" in the way that film is real, doesn't mean that it isn't emotionally real.

But do remember that you're writing for a live performance, which means that it's usually better to choose style over fancy technical tricks. Playwright Jose Rivera, in the same lecture where he talked about exposition as an IV drip, told us that he tries to write at least one impossible thing in each play. Take advantage of the possibility for magic in the theatre, and you can make the impossible possible.

Musicals

Audiences love musicals. Music is an energizing force, and combined with a play, it can be a powerful, uplifting thing. Writing musicals could be a book in itself, but in this space I'll try at least to provide some quick tips.

A main difference between how plays and musicals are created is that while the play is the product of a single playwright (very rarely do you see more than one author's name on a non-musical), musicals usually involve more than one writer. That's because musicals have three major components.

The first part of the musical is the book, which is the story/plot, including stage directions and any non-musical dialogue. It most closely resembles a non-musical play, and it's the part of a musical usually written by a playwright. The other two parts are the music and the lyrics. Some playwrights also write the lyrics or even the music, or each of these elements could be written by a different writer. When I wrote *Day One*, a musical for teens that was one of my commissions through the Choate Rosemary Hall Summer Arts Conservatory, I wrote the book and the lyrics, but since I don't write music, obviously someone else was going to have to write it. That someone turned out to be a composing duo, James Balmer and Mary Nelson.

A key part of writing a musical, assuming you can't write the entire thing yourself, therefore, is finding people who share your enthusiasm for the project and with whom you get along. Sometimes, a playwright who wants to write a musical will do an outline of the book before bringing in the rest of the creative team, or sometimes they'll all be on board from the beginning. That's up to you. Either way, I strongly recommend that if you work with others on your musical, you should have a written agreement that details the creative and financial relationship.

Getting started on a musical is very much like getting started on a non-musical play. You still should do an outline of the story beforehand, though because you're writing a musical, it's not going to have just the major plot events: it also needs to have a breakdown of the planned songs.

You have two decisions to make that are unique to the musical form. One, you need to decide whether this is going to be a through-composed musical (*Les Miserables* by Schönberg and Boublil is an example of a musical where the music is continuous, and all the words are sung), or one where the music periodically stops so that non-musical dialogue can happen (for example, *My Fair Lady* by Lerner and Loewe). Two, if you choose a musical which combines spoken sections and songs, you have to decide where the songs will go. Of course, despite what your outline may say, you may get into writing the piece and realize that what seemed like a dialogue exchange really should be a song.

Just as dialogue serves two purposes, to develop the characters and move the story forward, so does a song. In fact, when you think about it, a song is just dialogue (i.e. lyrics) set to music. Songs, like scenes or monologues, have a beginning, middle and an end. That means they go somewhere; we're not in the same place in the story—or in our understanding of the character who is singing—as we were when the song started.

Ultimately, as the book writer and lyricist, your focus is—very much like it would be in a non-musical play—on telling a good story. You just have an added element, music, with which to work.

There is much more to writing a musical than this. For example, the composer needs to worry about such things as what vocal parts each of the characters will need to sing. Lyrics can vary greatly, with many different styles and rhyme schemes. What musical style will the show use, or will it combine many different types of music? Will it need an orchestra, or can it be produced with just a band? The best way to get a good understanding of musicals and the many possibilities that exist is to see and read/listen to as many as you can. Check out my recommendations in the **Suggested Reading List** (Appendix E).

Adaptations

Way back when I was talking about where ideas come from (Chapter 1), I mentioned adaptation, which is when a writer writes a play based on someone else's writing. Usually, adaptations are of books (mostly novels), though they can be of poems or even occasionally of movies (*The Producers* and *Little Shop of Horrors* were both movies before they went on to become successful musicals).

What makes writing an adaptation different from writing your own play from scratch? The biggest difference is that the story, or at least its idea, is someone else's. When I taught at The Haverford School, I directed the North American premiere of *Lord of the Flies*. *Lord of the Flies* was originally a novel by Sir William Golding (it subsequently became two movies as well), and Nigel Williams adapted it for the stage. Williams didn't have to come up with the story/plot of the play; Golding had already done it. Even some of the dialogue was taken directly from the novel.

So doing an adaptation is easy, right? Wrong. Adapting someone else's work for the stage takes a great deal of careful work. Read on to find out how you go about it.

The first thing that happens, of course, is that you read some novel (for example) and decide, "I really, really like this." And not only that, but "I think this novel would make a great play—and I'm the person to write it." You've found your source. You're excited, and you're all ready to get to work, but there's something you have to do first.

You have to get the rights. When someone writes a book or a poem or a play or a song or any other type of creative work, that work is automatically copyrighted. That means if you use it without permission, you're breaking the law. Copyright protection, however, expires at a certain time after the author's death (currently it's the life of the author plus 70 years, but those laws used to be different, so it depends on when the material in question was written or registered). If our novel is sufficiently old, it may be in what's called the "public domain." That means that you're free to do anything you want with it. But if the novel is still under copyright, you have to get the permission of the copyright holder before you do anything else.

Why is it important to get permission first? If you don't, no one can legally produce your play, and it could sit in a drawer or on your hard drive forever. That's a lot of effort for absolutely nothing. So get permission. Usually the first place to start is by contacting the publisher of the book. They will likely either contact the author for you, or point you in the right direction. If you get turned down, there's not much you can do. (In my experience, the reason they might say no is that someone else is already working on a play, or there's a movie coming out—sometimes rights can be complicated.) If they say yes—or if your novel is in the public domain to begin with—it's time to get to work!

Perhaps the biggest decision you need to make early on is how closely you're going to stick to the original material. *War of the Buttons* is based on a French novel, *La Guerre des Boutons*, written in 1909 by Louis Pergaud, who died shortly thereafter in the fighting in World War I: the novel is in the public domain. This meant that I didn't have to worry about sticking to the story, or getting anyone's permission to change things around a bit. So I did. I reset my play—instead of in a French village—in an American town whose main industry, an ice cream factory, had closed, sending the town to the brink of ruin. Instead of a war between the youth of two villages, I changed it into a war between the youth of the town and the students at the boarding school that is buying up the town piece by piece as people go bankrupt. I created completely new characters and new dialogue—really the only thing I kept was the central idea of the war and the fact that the characters cut the others' buttons off.

What I did is called a "free adaptation," meaning that I didn't stick closely to the original source material. On the other hand, what Nigel Williams did with *Lord of the Flies* is a more traditional adaptation, in that he follows the plot in the book fairly carefully, has all of the same characters and even some of Golding's dialogue. How do you choose your style of adaptation? If the work is under copyright, the author or author's agent may tell you what you're allowed to do. If the work is in the public domain, you can make whatever choices you think make for the best play.

One of the problems with novels in particular is that they're not always dramatic. There are often long descriptive passages that may be wonderful reading, but they won't play on a stage. I remember when my friend, noted stage director Scott Schwartz, started working on his adaptation of Willa Cather's *My Antonia*. He had to work very hard to create a story that was dramatic and not just descriptive (Scott's a talented guy, and in the end he did it).

Part of making the story work on stage in an adaptation is being selective. If you put every single scene from the novel into the play, the play would probably take days to perform, be extremely expensive to produce and incredibly boring. So you have to choose which scenes are the most dramatic, the most important in telling the story you want to tell. Put those on stage, and leave out the rest. That's not as simple as it sounds. You might find that a certain scene doesn't really work, and you'd like to leave it out—but it has one crucial moment or piece of information. How do you solve the problem? One way is to "borrow" what you need from that scene and find a way to put it into one that you're planning to keep. Even if you have to satisfy the rights holder, if your choices make sense, they'll likely be supportive (nothing is for certain).

Another issue of adapting for the stage is that your original source may have many more settings and characters than is practical for a stage play. What if there are twenty or thirty settings? Either you'll have to use suggested settings, or you'll have to make some choices about which settings you use. Perhaps a scene that's currently set in one place (e.g. outside on the lawn) could just as easily take place in the kitchen, with no loss of dramatic impact. Similarly, is every character necessary? If not, can you cut a few? It's also possible in many cases to use multiple casting, so that one actor plays more than one character. That way, theatres that want smaller casts can do so, while a school or a community theatre that wants a larger cast can do the play without multiple casting.

Finally, what about the dialogue? Is there dialogue in the original material that you can use? Many adaptations (like *Lord of the Flies*, mentioned earlier) use dialogue that is largely from the source. But in some cases, that's not possible, so you'll have to invent your own, or you may have to mix the two. As with any play you write from scratch, make sure the dialogue fits the character speaking it.

Adaptation can be difficult, but it can also be rewarding, as audiences love to see familiar works put on stage (think of how often adaptations of *A Christmas Carol* by Charles Dickens are produced during the holidays). Don't be afraid to give one a try.

EXERCISE: Adaptation

Take a fairy tale or other classic children's story (something short and in the public domain) and create a rough plan for how you'd turn it into a play. What settings would you use? What characters would be in it? Finally, create an outline for the scenes you'd put on stage. Love what you've got? Why not try writing it?!

The Truth about Writer's Block

Ready? Writer's block is a myth. It doesn't exist. You're probably thinking, "Wait a second—sometimes I get stuck and can't write anything. Isn't that writer's block?"

There are some days when you're writing—maybe you're in the middle of a play that you really, really love to write—and you can't wait to get up every day and get started. The words seem to flow right out of your pen or your computer, and the script almost writes itself. I remember when I was in college (undergraduate, not graduate school) and I had days where all I did was eat, sleep and write. I think I wrote the original version of what went on to become *Play's End* in a day. Twenty pages in a day. Well, maybe it was a day and a half, but it was something incredibly brief and concentrated, because the words threw themselves onto the paper. I don't do that anymore.

What happened? I got older, had to pay bills, worry about my own meals and deal with the business end of my writing (dealing with script requests, updating my websites, consulting on scripts for others, etc): life just gets more complicated. So what does that have to do with writer's block?

What some call "writer's block" is simply your body or mind's way of telling you that you're not ready to work on a particular scene or play. Maybe you haven't quite worked out how the scene should go in your head. Maybe there's a nagging plot or character question that you haven't answered, and you need to think about it more. Maybe you have to study for a math test (however unwelcome it may be) or clean your room. Personally, I have a hard time working in a lot of clutter (though you may thrive on it). In any case, taking a break from your play is not the end of the world.

But maybe you feel as if you can't afford to take a break. Maybe your play is an assignment, and it's due soon (hopefully not tomorrow). Or maybe you just really, really want to get yourself back on track. How do you do it?

There is no magic wand to wave that allows you to get back to work. But here are some possible remedies, in no particular order:

1. Make a list of the other things "on your plate." Clear your list (at least somewhat) and then see if you can go back and write.

2. Create a "writing time" for yourself, and make it a daily ritual. If you can't write your play, write something (anything) else. Just write.

3. Don't sit at your computer (or with your pad) to write until you know your first line.

4. Go "burn" some time and clear your mind. That could be going for a run (often a productive, solitary time for writers) or a walk, people-watching in a café, or doing chores around the house. Even a little television might not be so bad here. (Note that I said a little!)

5. Read a book or see a play. There's nothing like giving yourself the creative equivalent of Vitamin C.

6. Write a monologue for a character in your play. Don't worry about making it fit into the play. Just pick a random topic and have fun.

7. Similarly, start a conversation between two characters in your play, and once again don't worry about whether it fits somewhere. Assume you're just doing it as an exercise, and if it happens to get used later, that's a bonus.

8. Ask yourself if there's some other play or piece of writing you need to do first (assuming you have the freedom to do so). Maybe there's another script that's pressing harder on your mind.

9. If your writing problem stems from being stuck on some particular moment in your play, try talking it out with a supportive friend or mentor. (It's better if they ask you questions rather than try to give concrete suggestions—you want to write your play, not theirs, though more about that later.)

10. Try improv. Actors can be a great source of ideas. Get a few actor friends together, set up the scene, and let them play it out, with you recording (either audio or video) what happens. Try it as many times as you like, changing some element of the set-up each time, so that you get to see different choices played out in front of you. They might hit on something useful and help you jumpstart your creative engine. [Note: Make sure your actors understand that they don't get part-ownership in your play, just your thanks. Of course, showing your thanks by buying them some food or drink is a nice touch.]

11. Write it anyway. Usually we "block" because we're worried that what we're thinking of isn't good enough. Just get it on paper, however bad you think it may be, and you'll fix it when you rewrite.

Giving Your Play a Title

Our very first contact with any play is going to be its title, yet many playwrights don't pay enough attention to coming up with good ones. A good title can be one word long: *Harvey* (Mary Chase). Perfect for a play about a man who sees a six-foot tall white rabbit. Or it can be a whole bunch of words: *Sister Mary Ignatius Explains It All for You* (Christopher Durang) or *A Funny Thing Happened on the Way to the Forum* (book by Gelbart and Shevelove, music and lyrics by Sondheim), both of which set the tone for their respective works. The mother of all long titles is, of course, Arthur Kopit's *Oh Dad, Poor Dad, Mama's Hung You in the Closet and I'm Feeling So Sad.* When you have a play where the father is literally a stuffed corpse in the closet, what other title could you have?

Two questions to ask yourself about a possible title. Does it give a sense of what the play is about? Does it have some resonance beyond its literal meaning (in other words, does it have more than one meaning?)? If the answer to both is yes, you're in very good shape. *The Zoo Story*, which may be the perfectly constructed one-act, has such a title. On the one hand, Jerry literally has gone to the zoo, and the story of what happened there gradually unfolds as part of the play. At the same time, Peter has his own little zoo at home, and more powerfully, the play makes the point that we are the animals in our own human zoo. It's the meanings beyond the literal meaning that gives the title its heft.

The Homecoming. Happy Days. The Importance of Being Earnest. A Midsummer Night's Dream. The Chairs. How I Learned to Drive. All of these are great titles because they carry more weight in their words than just their surface meaning. Whenever possible, that is the kind of title for which you are looking.

Before you panic, you do not have to name your play before you start. Or you might come up with a title that is merely holding the place until something better comes along. Sometimes it takes writing the entire play—or even getting into the rewrite process—before the right title emerges. In fact, some movies start out as "The Untitled So and So Project" (usually the name of the star or the director) until they finally come up with the right title. So don't worry. Usually, when the right title comes along, it'll click into place and it'll "feel right."

Finishing Strong

When I was talking about starting a play, I mentioned the old wisdom that you should start as late as possible in the action and end as early as possible. Just as it's important to get off to a good start, it's important to end well. Ending a play or even a scene is like doing a landing in gymnastics: you need to nail it, because that's what the audience will most remember when they leave the theater.

Of course, remember that first drafts are not going to be perfect, so getting to the end is far better than sitting around waiting for the perfect ending to hit you. But, for example, in any given scene, it's usually best to skip the characters greeting each other (assume it already happened) or saying goodbye (we can assume they'll do that after we leave them—if they're going to at all). Just stick to the main action of the scene. It's better to end the scene leaving the audience wanting a little more, and giving them something to think about as you move to the next scene.

Ditto with the ending of the entire play. While obviously you don't want to leave the audience confused, there is no reason to explain every last detail of what happens to each character. You especially don't want to sum up any scenes, lessons, morals, etc. Telling everyone what they were supposed to get out of the play at the end is a big no-no. Why? One, when you start to lecture your audience, you're likely to lose them. People were engaged by the story you put on stage and the characters who were part of it—once that story ends, your play had better end as well. Two, a wonderful thing about theatre is that there's no reason why everyone has to see your play in the same way. It may mean one thing to the mother in the third row, while the high school senior sitting in the back gets something completely different out of it. Both of their experiences can be just as valid, and it's all those different experiences that make the process of staging a play in front of a live audience such an exciting one.

If we continue comparing a good play to a piece of music, think of the ending as the play's final note. That note might be a line of dialogue, an action, an image. For example, while it's technically not the very last line, Blanche delivers the final note of *A Streetcar Named Desire* by Tennessee Williams in her immortal, "I have always depended on the kindness of strangers," as she exits. Or in *Sleeping Walter*, a wonderful children's play by Matt Buchanan about a boy whose dreams are so much better than his real life that he refuses to wake up, the final note of the play is an action and an image all in one: Walter, the boy, closes the closet door on the characters who have populated his dreams, symbolically choosing to wake up and face the real world.

What is the last note you want the audience to hear? Something hopeful, upbeat? Dark? Unresolved? Choose your music with care, and your audience will long remember it.

Chapter 8

REWRITING

Why We Rewrite

You've typed those beautiful words, "blackout" and "end of play," on your first draft. It feels tremendous to finish a script, and it's something that not everyone can do. Now that you're finished, put your play aside for a few days or even a few weeks and take a breath. You've earned it.

But you're not done—not even close. The first draft is that initial burst of inspiration, the place where you pour out all of your ideas, everything that might be genius or that might be awful. The point is to get it down on paper (or on your computer). Like a diamond coming out of a mine, a first draft is raw and unpolished and may not look like much. But after a playwright crafts it—just like the diamond after it's cut and polished—it can really shine.

Whenever you write a play, expect to rewrite; it's part of the process of writing. In fact, you'll spend more time rewriting than you will writing the initial draft—sometimes much, much more. A little later, I'll talk about the development process of three different plays, *Ben*, *Dear Chuck* and *After Math*, but for now, suffice it to say that the time you spend working on a play can range from a few weeks or months for a shorter play to several years for a longer play. As a rule, longer plays take longer to "finish" because their structures are more complicated.

We rewrite for many reasons. Sometimes there are specific things about a play that don't work. For example, maybe the plot isn't believable, or the characters don't sound "right" when they speak. When something is broken, you have to fix it. Sometimes, however, you just want to make something that's good even better.

To help in the process of "fixing" your script and then making it "even better," we are going to follow two rewriting steps. First, we'll go through the **Troubleshooter's Checklist**, a series of questions you should ask yourself about your script. Then, we'll wander into the **Writer's Web**, where you'll learn how to make specific parts of your play even more enticing for an audience—so enticing that they can't help but be drawn into the world you've created.

But before we begin, let's talk about...

Recentering

Plays change as we write them. The characters or story may have moved in unexpected directions. Your ideas may have changed as you wrote. You may have changed as a person—especially when you're young, you're bombarded by new life experiences all the time, and every one will change you a little. The bottom line is that very often, the play we started writing isn't the one we finish writing.

That's where "recentering," a term my late mentor William Alfred used to use, comes in. Recentering is the process of going back to the beginning of the play and "making it one" with the end. For example, maybe when you started writing, you thought that Jimmy wanted to be a star quarterback, but by the end of your process, you realized that the play is really about Jimmy's need for his father to come back. Your job as you recenter is to give the play little nudges (never obvious ones) so that everything Jimmy does is about making that happen. It's like taking a thread and making sure to weave it all the way through.

While you're giving that some thought, it's time to open up our very own play tune-up shop. It's the...

The Troubleshooter's Checklist

I'm a big believer in asking the playwright questions about the play as a way of helping the playwright write the play she wants to write— not the play I want to write. Ask yourself these questions as you enter the revision process—answer them honestly—and help yourself to a better play.

Character

Is each character distinct and well-developed?   Is each character's speech consistent with his background and education?

Is each character's behavior believable?

Does each character have a unique position in the play?   In other words, if two characters fulfill pretty much the same function, how can I make them different?   Or what if I removed one of them? Would anything be lost?

Are the relationships between the characters clearly established?

Do the characters change?   Static characters aren't as interesting to play.

Did I pick the characters' names for a reason?   As a sidenote, be careful of naming characters too similarly (e.g. James and Jack): it can be confusing.

Are these roles that actors will want to play? Does every actor have a moment to shine?

Structure and Conflict

Does the play have a clear conflict with a beginning, a middle and an end? Does the conflict build as the play goes on? Remember that two characters arguing isn't conflict: conflict is driven by characters trying to get what they want.

Does the play begin at the right point? Sometimes a play begins too early when it should begin in the middle of action.

Do the individual scenes begin too early or end too late? Usually, moments like "hello" and "goodbye" can be assumed, and the audience doesn't need to watch them every time.

Are the stakes high enough? It has to be crucial to each character that she gets what she wants.

Does every scene have conflict? Characters who desperately want things don't ever stop trying to get what they want.

Is there a ticking time bomb? Does the problem need to be solved urgently?

Is what happens in the play a result of choices the characters make, or do outside events dictate what happens? Strive for the former.

Dialogue
Have I eliminated ninety-nine percent of filler words like "well," "uh," "OK," "all right," etc.? Remember that while they are meant to make dialogue sound "realistic," they don't add anything.

Have I punctuated the dialogue accurately? Have I gotten someone else to read it out loud in front of me so that I can hear if the punctuation makes sense? It's super important to put periods, commas, dashes, semicolons and whatever else you're using where they belong. It's your best opportunity to communicate the rhythm of the lines to the actors.

Do I avoid dialogue which is only there to "tell" about the characters or the plot? Can I replace it with an action of some kind so I can show the audience what they need to know instead?

Does the length of the lines of dialogue vary?

Do I avoid having characters speak in "your turn, my turn" exchanges?

If there are long monologues, do they have a good reason for being there?

Stage Directions

Are the stage directions clear, concise and grammatical?

Do I use the stage directions to show what characters do, not to tell how they feel?

Do I write the stage directions in the "active voice"?

Is it clear in the stage directions which character is supposed to perform an action? Don't assume that it's obvious—usually, you should name the character specifically.

Have I avoided line readings (e.g. "angrily") except in crucial cases?

Have I given a specific time and a specific place (e.g. a living room, not merely inside a house) at the beginning of the play and at the beginning of each new scene?

Have I introduced each character with a one-line description (age, gender if it's not obvious, and a phrase of description) as we meet her within the script (not just on the cast of characters page)? This is crucial to help a potential director or producer determine who could be cast in the role, or simply to help a reader get a handle on your play.

Format

Is the play in proper format, with the character names, dialogue and stage directions all in the right place?

Is the speaker's name ever on one page, while the dialogue that goes with it is on another page? (If so, put them together.)

Are the scene/act headings centered?

Is my title page businesslike, without being overly flashy? Does it have the necessary contact information (name, address, phone number, email address) unless the submission guidelines tell me to do otherwise?

Do I have a draft number on my script? (I will discuss draft numbers in more detail later, but in short, a draft number tells you which version of the script it is.)

Other Important Questions

If the play requires research, do I have my facts straight?

Is the tone of the play consistent? You don't want a play to be a farce for the first ten pages and a family drama for the last ten.

Do I give the audience new information, or do I merely tell them things they already know? While a piece of information may be new to a character, it may not be new to the audience—and audiences get bored without new information. If I must repeat a piece of information (maybe another character has to hear it), is there a way I can add something to it, so that it's not exactly the same as what the audience heard before?

Every play is its own world. Are the rules of that world consistent?

Is my play's title both catchy and fitting?

Have I run a spell check? Have I proofread by reading aloud to make sure nothing has slipped through? Often, you can misspell a word into another correct word that your spell check won't detect. Have I given the play to someone else who has a good editor's eye?

I hope the Troubleshooter's Checklist has helped you address some of the problems in your play, and that you're starting to feel good about it. But why feel good about it when you can feel great?! Join me as we go where great scripts are made. Join me as we...

Step Into the Writer's Web

I learned about the Writer's Web from my friend, playwright, Ed Shockley. Here's why it works: specifics and details are what catch people's attention. A man may watch your play and be interested because a character in the play fixes cars, and so does he. Or a woman is a librarian, and you have a moment where a character talks about being locked in a library overnight with all of the books. Or maybe there's a drum, and another audience member loves that sound. Every detail you create is a strand of a web, and the more strands you weave, the better the chance that you'll draw the audience in, just like a spider and a fly.

Some of the tips mentioned in the Writer's Web have come up briefly in other sections of the book, but now I'll expand on them and focus on how to use them in your rewrites. As a practical note, rather than trying to weave every strand of the web at once, it's often easier to focus on one at a time: each time you go through your play, work on a different area (e.g. you might read for dialogue, and then the next time, read for sound). Ready? Here we go!

Place

Imagine two men conspiring to commit a crime. Not just a crime. A murder. That may already be enough to put us on the edge of our seats. But what if their intended victim is in the next room? Now, every noise matters.

Your setting should be more than just a place to hold the actors, which is why a therapist's office is nearly always a bad place to set anything. Why? Because chances are the conflict in question happened somewhere else, and the characters are only talking about it in the therapist's office. Instead, move them closer to the conflict. For example, have characters squabbling over an inheritance? Perhaps there's money rumored to be hidden in the casket. Want tension? Don't put it around a lawyer's conference table: set the play at the funeral home.

Remember, your setting should be just as much a part of the dramatic landscape as the actors in it.

Time of Day

Does your play take place at a specific time of day? Why did you choose that time? Does it maximize the tension?

Take the girl mentioned in passing in **The When** (Chapter 3). Imagine her out on the street after school, after midnight or during school. Each possibility brings something different to your play.

The first choice is the weakest. It's totally normal for a girl to be on the street after school. Maybe she's walking to a friend's house or waiting for her ride to ballet or a play date. Whatever her reason for being out there, there's nothing about that particular choice of time that adds tension to the play.

But if the girl is out alone after midnight, we immediately wonder what she's doing out alone so late. Has she run away from trouble, or is she in trouble herself? Is someone after her? Perhaps someone who was in her house? Do her parents let her run wild? We have questions, questions that engage us and keep us interested.

The last choice, the girl on the street during the school day, brings up more questions. Is she cutting school? If so, why? Or has she been excused? For what reason? Or maybe there's no school. (Remember, making it a weekend or a holiday is less interesting, whereas if there is a bomb threat or some other unusual reason for school to be closed, that would be interesting.) If she's out there on her own, do her parents know she's out there? Does the school? What are they doing about it?

More often than not, choosing a specific time of day will allow you to generate more dramatic tension. Try it!

Weather
Many plays seem to happen without weather. It's never mentioned, almost as if it's "neutral," something that does not affect the action. But why does it have to be? Specific weather can create all sorts of tension. What if your play is set during a severe drought (e.g. the stage adaptation of Steinbeck's *Grapes of Wrath*)? What if your characters live on a farm, and if it doesn't rain soon, they may lose that farm?

What if a woman is in labor—a tense enough situation—and she's snowed in at a restaurant during a blizzard? What if a couple is trapped inside an elevator during a heat wave? Earthquakes, tornadoes, roving thunderstorms that drench everyone in sight, lightning strikes, hail the size of golf balls, typhoons, flash floods— the possibilities are limitless. Remember that the weather doesn't always have to be extreme to add dimension and atmosphere to your play, influencing such choices of lighting (imagine the darkness outside when it's stormy), sound (rain pitter pattering on the windows or lightning crackling or wind blowing) or costume (you don't wear the same clothing in the summer heat as you do in a cold winter). And no, you don't need to make it rain onstage; the suggestion of weather is enough.

Character

If you've ever done any acting, ask yourself if you've read or seen a play and said to yourself, "I wish I could play that character." Part of writing great plays is writing great roles, roles that actors want to play. That's not hard to do when a character is the lead, but what about when a character only has a few lines, or has five minutes of stage time? The secret to making smaller roles desirable is to give every character a "moment." That moment might be a zinger of a one-liner, or perhaps some particular piece of business that everyone will remember. For example, while they're relatively smaller roles, the two mobsters in *Kiss Me Kate* (book by Bella and Samuel Spewack, music and lyrics by Cole Porter) steal the show with their musical number, "Brush Up Your Shakespeare." Just remember that every actor wants to shine!

Another question to ask yourself, building on the police files we created back in Chapter 2, is whether the characters have histories with each other. What if two characters went to school together? Or grew up in the same neighborhood? Or were both passengers in a car accident in which the driver died? How would that affect them in the present? It certainly provides context to their relationship (and thus will make their dialogue more high-context). How does that history affect the way they behave toward each other now?

Disability

Just like with the weather, we assume that every character in our play is physically neutral: we take for granted that they can enter and exit without problem, see and hear everything they need to, etc. But what if a character has a particular physical challenge? Take the example of Kattrin in Brecht's *Mother Courage*. She is mute. On a daily basis, it's one more obstacle to overcome, but it hits home with particular poignancy when, unable to cry out for help, she beats her drum to warn the town of Halle that the soldiers are coming.

Disabilities come in all shapes, sizes and degrees. A lisp or a stutter falls on one side of the spectrum, while someone like Helen Keller, who was blind, deaf and mute (her story is dramatized in *The Miracle*

Worker by William Gibson), is on the other. Disabilities can be temporary ones like a broken elbow or a sprain that requires crutches, or something much more permanent, like the leglessness of Nell and Nagg in *Endgame* by Beckett. Illness also constitutes a form of disability—for example, Edmund's chronic tuberculosis in *Long Day's Journey into Night* (O'Neill) has a substantial impact on the lives of him and his family, as does his mother's addiction to morphine. No matter what disability you choose, it can help you create a character who must overcome unique obstacles.

Absent Character
When we think about tension and conflict on stage, we usually picture confrontations. Two characters go toe-to-toe, using every tactic at their disposal, be it verbal or physical, to get the upper hand. And we're right there, watching them go at it. But some of the most powerful presences in all of theatre have been, in fact, absences.

The classic example is Godot in *Waiting for Godot*, Beckett's classic absurdist play. Vladimir and Estragon wait on a country road for Godot, a character they've never met. They believe that his arrival will be the solution to all of their problems, but in the meantime, they wait endlessly for him, afraid to leave their spot for fear of missing him. By the end of the play, nothing has changed. They're still there, and they're still waiting for Godot. An absent character controls everything.

We never meet the man whose coin collection the thieves plot to steal in *American Buffalo* (Mamet), and George and Martha in *Who's Afraid of Virginia Woolf* (Albee) not only battle over a son who never appears, but he's not even real. The weight of the Tyrones' dead child weighs heavily on them all in *Long Day's Journey into Night* (O'Neill), and a similarly dead father affects every moment in Ibsen's *Ghosts*. Despite never being physically on stage, all of these absent figures are nevertheless "characters."

Creating absent characters is a way to expand your play without needing a larger cast or more settings. It lets your audience know that there is a rich world going on beyond what they see on stage, and it opens up your work to many possibilities, both in and out of your view. So add that absence and watch your play open up.

Gender

Probably because I'm a guy, most of my lead characters are men. Considering that most of the "canon" (the plays people study in school) is written by dead white males, that's true of many of the plays you'll read in school. It doesn't make them bad plays, but for many of us, gender is an untapped resource.

Ask yourself, for example, what you would lose if you changed one of the men in your play to a woman? What would you gain? A son takes up boxing to show that he's a man in his father's eyes. Not an uncommon story. But what if the son were a daughter? (There was a feature series in the *Los Angeles Times* about just such a relationship.) How would that change the character, her behavior, her history and her relationships with the other characters in the play? Likewise, what if a victim of sexual harassment or abuse, usually female, were male?

Should you rush to change all of your characters' genders? Do you have to make a major issue of gender? Nope. It may not be your thing, and that's fine. But, for example, many men are accused of writing female characters that are more neutral than female. In other words, it's as if the writer just decided that "this one is a woman." Instead, pay attention to gender by endowing your characters with attributes that make them uniquely male or female. I understand that it's hard to know as much about the opposite gender as your own, but like any topic, you can research it by talking to your female friends (or vice versa if you're a female writer), observing and reading.

Race and Ethnicity

The dead white males also have a lot to do with why we often write plays that are race-neutral, with the assumption being that the characters are probably white. On the other side of the coin are playwrights like Suzan-Lori Parks or Amiri Baraka who make race an issue in their plays. But whether or not you want to focus on race, you don't need to ignore it either.

What if you take your play out of race-neutral? How would it change if a character is of a specific racial group? What if he's Asian and living in a black neighborhood? Or she's a Latino woman running a largely white, male office? Of course, the one big advantage of truly race-neutral characters is that they're easier to cast, so be aware that if you make a character race-specific, you now need an actor of a specific race to play the role.

What if the issue isn't skin color and race but rather one of ethnicity? In my free adaptation of *War of the Buttons*, one of the characters is a refugee from Bosnia. In fact, what if a Bosnian and a Serb immigrant, representatives of two groups with a long history of tension between them, were next-door neighbors in their new hometown of Chicago? Further, what if their recent arrival means they have language problems, and the only people who understand them are each other? Or what if a shopkeeper looks like an Arab but is, in fact, a Sikh?

Like gender, race and ethnicity are additional tools to diversify your play and introduce different cultures and a greater sense that there's a world out there.

Plot

It's great that your play is well-constructed. But you don't want it to become predictable. Feel like everyone knows what's coming next? Throw in a twist: make a character do something unexpected.

For example, in my play *Ben*, Ben is a homeless teenager who spends much of the play trying to get Baxter, the restaurant owner, to give him money. He begs for it and then offers to do all kinds of jobs around the restaurant. When he finally seems to be on the right track and Baxter offers to let him sleep at the restaurant, Ben trashes the place. Why would he do that? Up to this point, he hasn't seemed like that kind of kid at all. And yet he did it, so he must be. This twist engages the audience in trying to figure out why. As the writer, your job is to make it credible.

One thing to remember about plot is that you don't need to come up with some deep-seated psychological reason to justify a character's every action. What makes people interesting is that sometimes they just do things. Why does Ben trash the restaurant? Because he does. Sometimes a character's action is its own justification.

So the next time you want to shake up a play that feels "pat," throw in a plot surprise. You may just surprise yourself.

Dialogue

Do the characters all tend to sound the same, or does each character have a distinctive speech pattern? For example, an attractive woman passes two men. Bobby sees her and observes, "That's a very attractive woman." His pal Felix exclaims, "Somebody help me—a sweet ray of sunshine just blinded my eyes." We can tell these two apart with our eyes closed, just from their word choices. You may be thinking that Felix's dialogue is "better," more exciting, but remember that it's the variety of speech in the play that makes him stand out and be interesting.

Also, what if a character is from a particular region? In different parts of any country, people may use different words to describe the same thing. For example, what may be "soda" to me may be "pop" to you.

Another dialogue technique is to give a character a catchphrase, something he repeats. It adds texture to the dialogue, and often gives us a little insight into their psyche. For example, in *The Iceman Cometh* (Eugene O'Neill), Hugo's periodic refrain is "The days grow hot, O Babylon. Tis cool beneath the willow trees."

Subtext

Subtext, as I mentioned briefly in the discussion of **Levels of Dialogue**, is what's below the text, otherwise known as "what they really mean." For example, a character might say, "It's a nice day out." Many times in "real life," when we say something like this, we're doing it to fill the space; we're making small talk. But in a play, every line needs to count. How can "it's a nice day out" have a meaning "below the text"? Imagine two characters, Biff and Buff, in the midst of a heated conversation in the kitchen when a third, Tuff, wanders in.

BIFF

It's a nice day out, Tuff.

TUFF

Yeah, it is.

BUFF

He said it's a nice day. Outside.

TUFF

Yeah, I know. I was just out.

BIFF

You don't want to be inside on such a nice day. It might not be healthy.

Yes, Biff and Buff are telling Tuff (who agrees) that it's a nice day. But Biff and Buff aren't really talking about the weather. Instead, what they mean with their indirect dialogue is "Tuff, you shouldn't be here. You'd better go outside now, or something bad is going to happen to you." With subtext, ordinary-seeming dialogue can pack a real punch. So add some subtext, and punch up your play!

Names

Just like with play titles, names of characters and places in your play are another way to add resonance. Sure, sometimes we just like the way a word sounds, but what if it's more than just a pretty sound?

Take Prior Walter in *Angels in America* (Tony Kushner). It's no mistake that he's named Prior (meaning "before")—he even refers to it in the play. Or what about Happy in Arthur Miller's *Death of a*

Salesman? That's a name loaded with irony. In fact, some plays go so far as to be entirely filled with characters whose names are allegorical. Look at *Everyman*.

Picking a name with more than just face value is a way to add weight to your play and endow it with additional meaning. And these names are not limited to character names. Imagine a town named End of the Line, or Pleasantville. Yes, they both function as literal names, but they're much more than that, thus enriching your play.

Set

Sometimes it's enough to say "a restaurant" and leave the set to the production team to figure out. *Waiting for Godot* has done perfectly well with "A country road. A tree." Sometimes this may be the best choice. But a set offers rich possibilities for your play.

For example, imagine a living room decorated with animal trophy heads and a gun collection. What does this say about its owners? Or what if there is a realistic kitchen, only it's missing one key element—perhaps there is no sink. How do the characters live without it? Do they notice it's not there? Or maybe there's a particular portrait that occupies center stage—perhaps it's some famous ancestor, or even one of the characters. Or "Yankee Go Home" might be spray-painted on a wall.

Of course you don't want to call for a set that is impossibly expensive or difficult to create, but do not ignore the opportunity to strengthen the visual elements of your setting.

Costume

What are your characters wearing? Often, playwrights leave these decisions to directors and costume designers, but costumes are another way to make your characters stand out.

The right choice of attire can communicate visually all sorts of information about a character's position and personal habits and preferences, even her state of mind. Imagine Mary Tyrone descending the stairs like a ghost in her wedding dress in *Long Day's Journey into Night*, or Bottom transformed by a donkey's head in Shakespeare's *A Midsummer Night's Dream*. Costumes are an integral part of the stage picture—don't miss this opportunity to let your voice be heard about what you want that picture to look like.

Sound and Music
No matter how wonderful the words in your play or the voices of the actors who breathe life into them, it's nice to break them up. We've been talking about plays in musical terms, and adding sound or actual music is a way to increase the number of instruments at your disposal.

Sound spans a wide range of possibilities. There are sounds which the actors make themselves. Examples include a character who is pounding nails with a hammer, banging on a garbage can or even splashing around in a kiddie pool.

Then there are the sounds that are created by the designer and run on a sound system. That could be the sniper fire in *Little Murders* by Jules Feiffer, or the constant sound of tow trucks driving by in my own *Shining Sea*. Both sounds are an integral part of the plot, and they make the play a fuller experience for the audience. They don't hurt the tension either.

You can also use real music in your play (I'm not talking about a musical). It could be Gabe sounding his trumpet at the end of *Fences*, or songs played over the sound system. Some playwrights or productions will get a composer to score original music for a show, or a play may call for the use of existing songs. While you should be aware that specific songs may be difficult to include because of copyright issues (unless you are writing new ones), there is nothing wrong with suggesting a song "with the feel of 'Bridge over Troubled Waters'," or words to that effect. No matter how you use them, sound or music can only add to the richness of your play.

Lights

What colors do you see for the stage? Is the light supposed to be indoor (e.g. lamps inside a house) or outdoor (e.g. sunlight, moonlight, a street lamp)? Anything unusual about the light source? Perhaps there's lightning or the glow of a forest fire burning in the distance. What if the power goes out and there are candles or flashlights?

Again, you're not replacing the lighting designer (remember that not all productions have separate designers)—you're just giving them more with which to work. Since things like the choice of color affect the mood of the play, there's nothing wrong with voicing your desires. How you use the light is one more way to make your play visually enticing... Anybody have a light?

Props

Israel Horovitz's *The Former One-on-One Basketball Champion* has, as you can guess, a basketball in a central role. Harold Pinter has an extremely effective scene involving a plain old glass of water in *The Homecoming*. In my own dark comedy *Pepperoni Apocalypse*, a pizza box, never opened, might just bring about the end of the world.

Having too many props in a play can be a nightmare, as it forces your production staff to spend much of its time tracking them down, and then the rest of it making sure they don't get lost. But having a few choice objects that figure in the dramatic action benefits your play in two key ways. One, a prop is a potential point of negotiation. Who controls it? For what purpose? Who else wants it? Two, props are tangible, physical things, which means that they add to the visual palate formed by the set, lights, costumes and actors.

Have a play that largely consists of people moving around empty-handed? Add a prop, and see how its presence affects them.

A Secret
Once an audience knows everything about the world of a play and its characters, your play had better be over. If we know everything, there's no reason for us to pay attention anymore. So what's the secret to keeping an audience hooked and digging for more? The secret is just that: a secret.

I have a one-act play, *You're Next*, in which Jay, a teenage boy, is the target of a school bully. Peter, his friend, brings a gun to school for Jay to use to scare the bully. As the play goes on, Peter's desperation for Jay to use the gun—despite Jay's reluctance—grows considerably. As an audience, we're digging, trying to figure out what is the missing puzzle piece to justify Peter's near obsession with Jay scaring off the bully. Peter has a secret, only revealed when he has no other choice: the bully has told him that he, Peter, is next. He's too afraid to use the gun himself and believes Jay using it is his only hope.

Or take Jerry in Albee's *The Zoo Story*. He made a decision at the zoo that he was going to find someone and talk to him until he got the desired result, his own death. If he had revealed "what happened at the zoo" at the beginning of the play, Peter would have run off, and Jerry would not have gotten what he wanted. And in the meantime, the audience watches, trying to figure out where Jerry's dialogue is leading them.

Sprinkle in some secrets, and bring the audience along for a ride.

Storytelling
I've talked many times about the idea of your play as a piece of music. If every note sounds the same, it becomes nothing more than "white noise" that will put us to sleep. One way to avoid that is through storytelling.

Storytelling, by its very nature, lets us escape from the moment and takes us to another place, a place in our minds where we "watch" the story unfold—think of it as sitting around the campfire on a warm summer night. Stories can be lyrical, beautiful and very sensory, in contrast to the harsh sounds and rhythms of conflict. It's more likely that stories will be longer, slower moments, while pure conflict tends to be staccato.

August Wilson is a master storyteller. In *The Piano Lesson*, the stories become little islands in the play. They give the audience a break from typical back and forth dialogue, and at the same time, they develop the world of the play and its characters (they're third-level dialogue, as discussed in Chapter 5). And more than that, stories can give the world you've created a sense of history. Written properly, they're a wonderful counterpoint to the rest of the music in your play.

Religion and Philosophy
Too often, as we construct our characters, we focus only on what they "do" (e.g. Mike is a lawyer) or their situation (e.g. Jennifer is leaving town). But what do your characters believe? What if a character were a devout Christian or a Jew or a Buddhist or a Moslem? How would that affect the way she lived her life, or her dealings with other characters?

Of course, belief systems are not only religious in nature. Think of such philosophers as Thoreau and Emerson, or such movements as existentialism or Dadaism. These belief systems can enrich a character and a play in much the same way.

Whatever the choice of religion or philosophy, the fact is that it connects the characters to something larger than just what we see on stage. Bigger, in this case, is better.

Myth and Legend
Every culture has its own set of myths and legends, from the Greek heroes and gods to the Knights of the Round Table to the plethora of gods, heroes and spirits of African and Asian mythologies. How would their presence—literal or figurative—in your play lend it weight?

Myths and legends can connect characters to a culture or belief system in the same way as a religion or a philosophy. For example, have these myths or legends caused any superstitions to arise? If so, how does that affect the behavior of the characters? What if a character believes himself cursed? What does he do to throw off the curse? Or does he give up, believing that fighting the curse is hopeless?

Maybe a little inn is always busy because it's believed to be the last inn at which George Washington ever slept. What if it's not true? What might the innkeeper do to keep his secret? Or what if it *is* true? What might it be like to sleep in George Washington's old room, or even in his bed? Do people believe there's something magical about the experience?

Even if a myth or legend isn't a major plot component, it's another opportunity to bring the larger world into your play.

Magic and the Supernatural

In *Hamlet*, the ghost of Hamlet's murdered father returns to cry for revenge. Jose Rivera's *Marisol* has guardian angels roaming the world turning people to salt to protect their charges. In *Angels in America* (Tony Kushner), the ghost of Ethel Rosenberg guides Louis through the Kaddish, the Jewish prayer for the dead that he doesn't even know.

Does your play have room for a touch of the supernatural, or a little magic? Perhaps there are actual angels or ghosts or witches. Or instead, maybe there's simply some event that cannot be explained. Maybe a cancer patient miraculously heals, or a long broken television suddenly starts playing reruns of old shows. Whatever it is, there may be no logical explanation, and that opens a door to a larger universe in which your play can exist.

Rituals

When most people think of rituals, they think of magical rites or religious ceremonies. But rituals are usually just common, everyday things that we do. For example, brushing your teeth is a ritual you perform at least twice (we hope) each day. Maybe another person always takes a morning walk or reads the newspaper or phones her granddaughter. Giving characters rituals is a way of filling in and enriching their lives. What are your characters' rituals?

Just as important as a ritual is disrupting one. What if the woman who always phones her granddaughter on Wednesday at 10 AM doesn't make the call that morning? What will her granddaughter think? What happened to prevent her from making the call? What if she suddenly decided that she wasn't going to do it anymore? What reaction would that cause? What if the man who takes his morning walk suddenly finds that his peaceful park has been turned into a construction site? How will he react? Either of those disrupted rituals will enrich—or even create—a play.

Theme and Thesis

So many writers want to write plays "about" something. That's not a bad thing, but starting in that place can be dangerous. It often leads to plays that are preachy, plays in which the characters are largely just the author's ideas in disguise and are, at best, two-dimensional. The worst culprits are often those who write for young people, talking down to them and providing "moral instruction" that, for whatever its other values, is poorly constructed from a dramatic sense.

Rather than try to write in themes from the start, I don't worry about them. But since this is a section about rewriting, it's finally time to talk theme. For me, the best plays are ones that don't tell the audience what to think, but that instead open up possibilities. For example, *The Glass Menagerie* (Tennessee Williams) and *The Iceman Cometh* (O'Neill) examine the illusions people create for themselves, whereas *The Bald Soprano* (Ionesco) calls into question how we communicate with each other, or whether we really are communicating at all.

Almost always, as I write a first draft, themes emerge on their own. Once you see certain themes emerging, if they're themes you want in your work, you can thread them through the entire play. In *Ben*, it eventually became clear that an issue I was wrestling with was our search for connection. Once I saw that theme emerging, I went back through the play and gave each character some particular attempt at connection. (The trick is not to be too obvious or heavy-handed about it.) But I didn't do that until the play revealed what it was about; I didn't force it.

The bottom line is that if you can use theme to open the door to larger issues of human behavior and existence without limiting the discussion, that's a door worth opening.

Chapter 9

THE NEXT STEP

What to Do With Your "Finished" Play?

You've finished your first draft. You've proofread it, running a spell check to catch the obvious errors and then proofed "by hand" to catch the errors spell check doesn't catch (for example, if you misspell a word into another word, like your and you're, it's and its). You've applied the **Troubleshooter's Checklist** and the **Writer's Web** to rewrite and shape your script.

You may go through multiple drafts as you rewrite. Personally, I like a clean, printed copy of the script each time I do a new rewrite (e.g. I've done the "character" rewrites, and I want to print a new copy before I move on to "rituals"). It gives me a feeling of order and of progress. To avoid wasting a truckload of paper, however, try using the other side of paper that's already been printed on (don't do this, of course, if you're sending the script to someone else). So now what?

1. When you feel that you've done all you can do on your own, give the script to someone you trust. If you don't have anyone in whose judgment you feel confident, I'd skip this step, because bad feedback is worse than no feedback.

Quick Tip: Draft Numbers
Save each draft as a different number. That way, there's no question about which draft is the current one. For example, your first version might be *Dear Chuck* 1.1, and the first rewrite might be 1.2. My own system is to go up a whole number (e.g. 1.1 to 2.1) if there's been a reading/production and a major rewrite, and to go up a .1 (e.g. 1.1 to 1.2) when there's been a rewrite that's significant but not on the level of a whole-number shift. I also use .01 when I've done a little polish (e.g. 1.1 to 1.11) that's made a small change in the script, but nothing substantial. It's not as complicated as it probably sounds. Find the system that works for you. I advise against using dates, because when you submit your work, if the date is very new, the producer will think you rushed to get the play out, and if it's very old, they'll wonder why it's been lying around: you can't win, so stick with draft numbers.

Quick Tip Too: Back It Up!
There is nothing more frustrating than losing your script in a computer crash. To avoid this, back up your play regularly somewhere other than your hard drive. You could burn it to a CD or DVD (or a floppy disk or zip drive—whatever you have available), or keep it in cyberspace if you have a website. Having a printed copy is a good idea, too. Ideally, don't keep everything at one location (i.e. use either a virtual location or have a parent keep a disk at work), in case of fire, burglary, etc.

Important: Go With Your Gut
When you give your script to someone for feedback, there is no law that says you must act on every note they give. Follow your instincts. If the comment feels right to you—for me, "feels right" means that the comment was something I was already thinking but was afraid to admit to myself—listen to it. If it doesn't feel right, disregard it. And remember that even smart people can be wrong about a script. For example, when I was in graduate school, a very reputable director on the faculty steered a student playwright completely wrong, simply because he didn't understand her play. It happens.

2. The next step is a sit-down reading (sometimes called a "table reading"). Get a group of actors (or even a group of your friends) together. There is no staging and no memorizing: it's just about hearing the words out loud. I'll usually hear some lines that don't sound right and make adjustments. If you'd like, gather a few people whose feedback you trust as the "audience," but you don't need to. It can be just you and the actors. For all readings, it's best to give the actors the script ahead of time so they can practice and not trip over the words.

3. Have a directed, rehearsed reading. To do this, you need a director and actors. They should have a few rehearsals (the reading should be script-in-hand so that the actors get the words right). Often, this kind of reading is done with music stands, or very simple up and down staging (i.e. the actors who are in the scene stand). You may wish to invite an audience, or sometimes it's better to work through the script with just the actors and the director. If you do invite an audience, invite an audience that you think will be constructive.

4. Have a staged reading in a public setting with a more general audience. This type of reading will have some minimal staging, but the focus should still be on your text—don't get distracted by complex staging, props or other design elements. Have a directed post-show discussion to get feedback if you like. In brief (I'll spend more time on this later), that means that someone—usually the director or a dramaturg (a script advisor for playwrights)—moderates the conversation so that it's useful and doesn't go off in the wrong direction.

5. If you have the opportunity, have a more fully realized production (using props and costumes, minimal set, memorized lines—sometimes called a workshop production) at your school or in a similarly "safe" place. At productions of my work (or even at readings), I watch the audience—seeing how they react during the performance gives me clues as to what is working and what isn't.

Does every play go through this entire process? Of course not. Let me use three of my plays as examples:

I wrote the first draft of *Ben* when I was an undergraduate at Harvard. The original incarnation of the script had a workshop production there (directed by now-Broadway director Scott Schwartz). It was a great experience, and afterward, I rewrote the script considerably, cutting a half-hour in running time and focusing the story. Since then, it's had a number of readings, including two at Playwrights Theatre of New Jersey, one of which was around a table, and the other was a "concert reading" (using music stands—like #3 above). Over the years, the play has undergone substantial changes—for example, the cast, which used to require 10 actors, now only needs 7. While *Ben* has been recognized with several awards and is supposed to have another reading out here in Los Angeles, it awaits its first full professional production.

Dear Chuck was a commission from the Choate Rosemary Hall Summer Arts Conservatory. I wrote the first draft in just a few weeks, and by the end of the summer that I was in residence, we did an elaborate staged reading/workshop of it. The actors were on book (mostly), but there was considerable staging, as well as props, minimal lighting and costumes, and wooden blocks as the set. I did some relatively minor rewriting after that, and it had a school production in Canada. Shortly thereafter, Eldridge Publishing published it.

After Math had the least development of the three. I wrote the first draft in a month or two, and because it was written specifically for teen actors (as was *Dear Chuck*) and I had been having success getting published in that market, I decided to go right to publication. I got a few actor friends together, did a reading around my dining room table, did some rewriting (including adding a few scenes, as I wanted the script to be in the 30-35 minute range so that it would be a good contest piece), and then submitted it to publishers. I had multiple offers on it, and I chose Playscripts, Inc.

The bottom line is that every script's path to success is different. The steps in the "What to Do With Your 'Finished' Play" process are there to give you a picture of the possibilities. Choose as many of them as you need, and feel free to back-track if you feel that your play needs more work. When you think that your script is ready (don't rush!), it's time to look at contests and other submission opportunities for young writers (see Appendix C). Good luck!

I Can't Say It Enough!!!
Sloppy scripts—with misspelled words, poorly punctuated sentences, handwritten changes—are the mark of sloppy writing. Many readers are instructed to put them down, and this can kill your relationship with a theatre. Your script is your face. Don't show it until it's clean!!

How to Have a Useful Play Reading...and How to Survive It!

Because theatres have less and less money, there has been a significant trend toward having fewer fully-realized productions and more readings (which are much cheaper to produce). These may be table readings or more fully staged ones that feel as if they're caught halfway between a reading and a full production. Readings, at their best, represent an opportunity for writers to develop their plays and improve them, or even to show them off to potential producers.

There are three possible purposes for readings. The first is the developmental reading, which is for the writer: it's meant to help the playwright improve her work. The second is the backers' audition, which is a showcase for the play in front of potential producers. The third is the "reading as production," which is basically the theatre's way of saying that "we want to produce your play, only we don't have the money, so we're going to do this nifty reading in front of an audience—and we're even going to have a few props and have the actors move around a bit."

We're going to concentrate on the first type of reading, the one which exists to help you make the script better, as that's one you might even decide to hold yourself.

The Reading

Remember that the actors will be "on book" (not memorized), so it's best to find actors who can read (or potentially cold/sight-read if they haven't had much time with the script) fluently. It doesn't matter if they're not an exact fit for the role, as it's a reading and not a production.

I repeat: do not have actors memorize. It's about your words, so you want to make sure they get them right.

Avoid elaborate staging or movement; it's hard to do it with a book in hand, and again, it's about the text, the words. As I mentioned previously, one way I've seen readings done is to have actors who are in a particular scene stand at music stands in front, while the others stay seated in back.

Similarly, avoid elaborate lighting (usually up and down is plenty), sound, costumes or props. This is important not only to avoid "clutter," but also because if you get too elaborate, the audience starts to confuse the reading with a production, which will take the focus off the text and cause them to judge your play differently.

The Post-Reading Discussion

After most readings, there will be a discussion. These can be nerve-wracking for playwrights, because you're sitting up there, feeling naked, and you have no idea whether those in attendance are going to open fire on your script and destroy your baby. So how do you survive this thing and actually make it useful? Here are a series of tips, both for you as a playwright and for those who may be participating on the audience side.

The most important thing to understand is that <u>YOU ARE NOT YOUR PLAY. YOUR PLAY IS NOT YOU. NEVER TAKE CRITICISM OF YOUR PLAY AS A CRITICISM OF YOU AS A PERSON</u>. I cannot emphasize this enough. People are there to talk about a script, not a person. You are not your play. Your play doesn't sleep in your bed, eat your food, get yelled at by your parents (hopefully neither do you—at least not much), etc. So do not confuse the two.

It's best that your director (or another knowledgeable person) act as moderator, so you can just listen.

Prepare for the discussion in advance by coming up with a list of questions that you would like answered. You can give these questions to the moderator to ask for you. For example, you might want to know, "Is it clear that Jake wants to leave in Scene 3?" Or another, possibly better way to ask that same question is, "What did you think Jake wanted in Scene 3?" That way, you don't guide the audience in any way. When I moderate, I always begin on a positive note: "what did you like?" It helps put the playwright at ease, because he'll see that the audience actually did like some things about the play. Then I'll move on to "what didn't you understand?" and "what would you like to see more or less of?"

Take notes. When I'm the playwright, I write down everything said in the discussion, whether I think it's useful or not.

Be a silent author. Never defend your work or enter the discussion in any way, except to ask questions if you don't understand a comment. If you don't agree with a comment or a suggestion, ignore it.

For the audience, questions are a great way to give feedback. Here's an example: I've just been to a reading of your new play, *Romeo and the Dog Catcher*. At the post-reading discussion I ask, "Why does Romeo buy a dog in Act II and then let it go in Act III?" You don't need to answer my question right now. In fact, it's better if you don't. Instead, write it down, and answer it for yourself later. The reason I'd rather ask you a question than give you a comment is that, given the same characters and circumstances, you and I wouldn't write the same play. No two people would. So by asking you a question, I give you the opportunity to answer it in a way that works for you and the play you're trying to write. You may decide that the answer to my question either doesn't matter or is already answered well enough in the play. Or you may decide that my question needs a better answer than the play currently gives, and rewrite—on your terms.

Why not answer my question then and there? One, because answering my question after the fact doesn't change the reality that seeing your play left me with a question, which is all that matters. Two, it slows down the discussion, and it's easy to go from answering questions to defending your play—and you don't want to go there. The important thing is to find out whether the audience got what you wanted out of your play.

Avoid prescriptive feedback. When I'm moderating, whenever someone starts to say, "I think you should..." I cut them off. It's important not to tell people what or how to write—that kind of feedback isn't helping them improve, but rather telling them how to write the play you would have written.

Have I ever given prescriptive feedback to the playwright after a play reading (or after reading a script)? If questions and descriptive comments (e.g. "I didn't understand why...") aren't working, and the playwright begs me to come up with something to illustrate my point, I will give a deliberately bad example and say, "Here's a bad example to show you what I mean. Come up with something that works for your play." For example, let's say we agree that the opening of your play, *Romeo and the Dog Catcher*, needs a jumpstart, but you have no idea how to go about it. When questions and descriptive comments fail, I cave in and give you an example: "What if the play opened with the Dog Catcher chasing Romeo around the stage with a giant net?" I don't necessarily want you to use my example (if you really love it, you can)—the point is for it to inspire you to come up your own idea, one that fits the play you want to write.

Finally, speaking as a playwright again, remind yourself that everyone is there because they're interested in your work, that writing a play is a long-haul process and that you knew you'd be rewriting after the reading. Feel free to take some time off and write something else, giving yourself time to digest the comments and get a little distance from your current play.

Conclusion

I hope that the lessons in *Young Playwrights 101* have been helpful. While there are five Appendices after this note filled with practical information (formatting, the business of writing, links to submission opportunities, sample query and cover letters and a reading list), this is, for all intents and purposes, the end of the main instructional part of the book. But before we go our separate ways, I want to offer a few final suggestions about growing as a playwright, both in the craft and in the business:

Be a theatregoer. You don't need to go to Broadway. Seeing almost anything is a learning experience (personally, I draw the line at junior high and elementary school plays, though junior high productions would be OK if you're still in junior high). Take advantage of local college productions and smaller professional companies (many of which have discounted student tickets), and be on the lookout for new play readings (many of which are free) at local playwrights organizations and at theatre companies. The more plays you see, the easier it is to see "how things work on stage."

Especially if you can't see a lot of plays (but even if you can), read them. To be a good playwright, you need to read good playwrights. Expose yourself to writers with different styles. To find out some plays I think you should read, check out the **Suggested Reading List** (Appendix E).

Meet local theatre people. Find out what companies are in your area and develop relationships with them. Find out if there is a local support organization for playwrights and get involved. For example, I co-chair the Alliance of Los Angeles Playwrights (http://www.LAPlaywrights.org), which has a special student membership. Most readings and productions come from relationships developed over time.

Use the internet. Create a website to publicize your work. Learn what sites will let you post information about your plays, what sites will link to your site, and where to look for playwriting opportunities (you'll find a bunch in Appendix C).

Learn your rights (see Appendix B), and don't let people walk all over you just to get a production. Start by joining The Dramatists Guild of America (http://www.dramatistsguild.com) or your equivalent national organization for playwrights.

Keep a little notebook or tape recorder around, and if you come across an interesting character or "life moment," make a note of it.

Finish a script? Start another one. Now. Writing a script is like giving birth, and the script is your baby. Our babies are always beautiful and perfect. In our eyes, they can do no wrong. But when you write something new, you make the new play your baby, and the first play becomes the older sibling, perhaps even a teenager. Now you have some distance to look at it critically, and we all know that teenagers are never perfect. And if you're sending out that first script to contests or theatres, writing something new sure beats waiting for the mail to arrive every afternoon.

Make it a point to do at least one thing each day to further your career. That one thing you do could be to write or outline a play, to send out a submission, to read a play or even just to think about one of your plays. But do something. You're not an "aspiring playwright." You're a playwright. So get out there and be one.

Be your own biggest fan. Don't be arrogant or unrealistic, but if you don't believe that you can do it, who will? At the same time, this is one of the toughest businesses in the world, so understand that rejection is part of the game. I have hundreds of rejection letters, and while some hurt more than others, after every one, I get up and keep right on going—because writing is what I love to do. And finally…

Write plays that shake—plays that shake with your energy and passion, plays that make us shake with laughter or shake us up. As a playwright, you have tremendous power to affect people in the very special way that only live theatre can do. Don't waste it writing plays that are essays or intellectual exercises in disguise, or plays that are wannabe sitcoms. Plays are meant to rock the world—sometimes just a tiny corner of it—so get to it.

About the Author

Jonathan Dorf has had his plays produced in more than thirty states, as well as in Canada, Europe and Asia. He has been a finalist for the Actors Theatre of Louisville Heideman Award, the Weinberger Playwright Residency, the Charlotte Repertory New Play Festival and the InterAct New Play Festival. His work has been seen at Playwrights Theatre of New Jersey, Ensemble Studio Theatre - LA, Moving Arts and the Pittsburgh New Works Festival, and he's had plays commissioned by the Walnut Street Theatre and the Choate Rosemary Hall Summer Arts Conservatory, where he served as playwright-in-residence for three years. His plays are published by Brooklyn Publishers, Eldridge Publishing and Playscripts, Inc., while his monologues are in collections by Meriwether and Smith & Kraus.

He is resident playwriting expert for Final Draft (for whose software he created the playwriting "Ask the Expert") and The Writers Store (author of Playwriting101.com and playwriting instructor at Writers University), the co-chair of the Alliance of Los Angeles Playwrights and the former managing director of the Philadelphia Dramatists Center. He headed the drama program at The Haverford School for six years and served as a playwriting mentor for Philadelphia Young Playwrights, in addition to teaching dramatic writing at the Walnut Street Theatre and the Wilma Theater. He has been a guest artist at over a dozen schools and youth theatres in the US and the UK, and he is a member of the Dramatists Guild of America and the Los Angeles-based Ariadne Group. He holds a BA in Dramatic Writing and Literature from Harvard University and an MFA in Playwriting from UCLA and works with playwrights, screenwriters and other writers worldwide as a consultant. He can be reached through his website at http://www.jondorf.com or via email at jon@jondorf.com.

Selected Plays by Jonathan Dorf

"Jon Dorf is the voice of this generation's high school student. He has captured the inner and outward struggles that confront today's youth and brings light to those issues that we deem important but are too afraid to broach. The significance of his work is far beyond that of his writing genius. It speaks to everyone on a personal level and gives a voice to a growing population that has so much to say. His plays have proven vital, not only to the growth of our young actors but also to the development of their young minds. We continue to use Jon's works here at Choate Rosemary Hall and look forward to his next creation."
- Paul Tines, Executive Director of the Paul Mellon Arts Center and Head of the Choate Rosemary Hall Arts Department

All of these plays are suitable for school-age actors and audiences. At the end of this list, you'll find the necessary web addresses and phone numbers to order perusal scripts. For a complete play listing and direct links to order information, please visit http://www.jondorf.com.

After Math
One-act seriocomedy. A student mysteriously disappears in the middle of math class. What happened? In a series of scenes and monologues, those left behind try to find some answers. But why is it they've only noticed him now that he's gone? Written specifically for teen actors. Available from Playscripts, Inc.

Beef Junkies
One-act dark comedy. A woman addicted to beef searches for her fix, and there's only one cow left on earth. Available from Brooklyn Publishers.

Crash Positions
Ten-minute comedy. When two passengers think their airplane is about to crash, comic mayhem ensues. Available from Brooklyn Publishers.

Day One
Full-length musical, with book and lyrics by Jonathan Dorf, music by James Balmer and Mary Nelson. Some people wish the high school years would last forever. Others would do anything to get them over with. What if they all had a chance to get their way? Written specifically for teen actors. Available from YouthPlays.com.

Dear Chuck
One-act seriocomedy. Through a series of scenes and monologues--everything from taking over the kiddie pool at the local swim club to dealing with a skinhead classmate--the play's eclectic assortment of teen characters, caught between being children and adults, search for their "Chuck," that elusive moment of knowing who you are. Written specifically for teen actors. Available from Eldridge Publishing.

From Shakespeare With Love?
One-act comedy. Four of the Bard's characters wait for an overdue flight to London. When Romeo reveals that he plans to revenge himself upon Shakespeare by killing him in a duel, it's up to the others—Titania, Viola and Antipholus—to save Shakespeare by convincing Romeo that Shakespeare "does indeed love love." Available from Eldridge Publishing.

Last Right Before the Void
Ten-minute comedy. A teenager hitchhikes along a highway that seems to disappear into a black hole in this offbeat short. Available from YouthPlays.com.

Le^{a}pers
Ten-minute comedy. When two jumpers end up on top of the same building, it's a fight to the finish. Available from YouthPlays.com.

Menagerie
Ten-minute comedy. A missing roommate. An eight year old thief on the loose. Sleep deprivation. A gift of a chicken. It all comes to a head on Valentine's Day. Available from Brooklyn Publishers.

Newt Gingrich Visits a Residential Youth Facility Not Near Omaha
Ten-minute drama. A pair of residents at a home for troubled teens wait for a photo op with Newt Gingrich. Written specifically for teen actors. Available from Brooklyn Publishers.

Now You See Me
A one-act seriocomic play about what happens when young people slip through the cracks, and what drives them to violence. Written specifically for teen actors. Available from Brooklyn Publishers.

Pepperoni Apocalypse
Ten-minute dark comedy. A pizza delivery man arrives at the exact moment a doomsday cult expects the world to end. Available from Brooklyn Publishers.

Play's End
One-act tragicomedy. A door-to-door gun salesman comes home from work to learn from his young son that "something happened today." Part of the *Gunplay* trilogy and available from Brooklyn Publishers.

Ticking
A gun disappears from the pot on the right rear burner in the Doe family kitchen, replaced by an egg. John Doe, traveling gun salesman, thinks his teenage son Jay has taken it, and he wants it back. Part of the *Gunplay* trilogy and available from YouthPlays.com.

Twisting Carol
A one-act comic slaughter of the Dickens classic. Young Ebenezer Scrooge dancing with a popsicle stick, a ghost named Bob, another ghost who thinks his name is Bob and a Tiny Tim who considers himself short but not tiny. Available from YouthPlays.com.

Whatever Happened to Godot?
Ten-minute comedy. The untold story—until now—of why Godot, one of the most famous characters in all of theatre, never showed up. Available from Brooklyn Publishers.

The White Pages
One-act comedy. A customer takes matters into his own hands when he discovers a used bookstore is removing the pages from classic books and replacing them with blank ones. Available from Brooklyn Publishers.

X Marks the Spot
Ten-minute comedy. A modern-day Moses and Zipporah (Mo and Zippy) try to rekindle their flagging romance with a trip to a middle-American burning bush. Available from Brooklyn Publishers.

Yard Wars
One-act comedy. A backyard wrestler traces his career as he wrestles with whether to continue in a match after suffering a concussion. One performer shifts in and out of ten different characters, or the roles can be broken up among several actors. Available from YouthPlays.com.

You're Next
One-act drama. A bullied teen brings an equalizer to school, but can he use it? Part of the *Gunplay* trilogy and available from YouthPlays.com.

Contact Information for Script Orders

Brooklyn Publishers   http://www.brookpub.com
Email: info@brookpub.com
Phone: 1-888-473-8521 (432-550-5532 outside the US)

Eldridge Publishing   http://www.histage.com
Email: info@histage.com
Phone: 1-800-HI-STAGE

Playscripts, Inc.   http://www.playscripts.com
Email: info@playscripts.com
Phone: 1-866-NEW-PLAY

YouthPlays.com   http://www.youthplays.com
Email: info@youthplays.com

Appendix A

FORMATTING YOUR PLAY

Formatting Basics

Presenting your script properly is crucial. As a reader, it's easy to get turned off to a script that isn't formatted correctly and that makes reading more difficult. Look at the example below, a tiny cutting from *Beef Junkies*, my play about a woman addicted to meat and looking for her fix. Does the format look familiar?

COWGIRL: I see a hamburger.
COWBOY: Where?
COWGIRL: *(points in the air not far away)* There.
COWBOY: Where?
COWGIRL: By the tree. In the bun. Can't you see it?
COWBOY: Is it very small?
COWGIRL: It's ten feet tall.

It's published play format. The problem many writers have is that they format their plays like the published scripts they've seen, not realizing that these condensed formats exist primarily for the publisher to save space (and therefore money)—and that they're not what theatres (at least in the United States—keep reading to find out about formats for Australia, Canada, France, New Zealand and the UK) want when you submit.

So what do theatres want? They want something called manuscript format, but unlike film, stage formats are not set in stone; there is what I'd call a certain amount of acceptable deviation. Frankly, the easiest thing to do is get a formatting program (none of them are perfect, but Final Draft is solid and getting better).

The font of choice for stage is either Courier or Times Roman, but anything clear and readable is acceptable. No cursive fonts.

Page margins are usually 1" on the top, bottom and on the right, but 1.5" on the left (because of hole punching/brads/binding, you need more space on the left).

Character names (those speaking) are either centered or left indented at a consistent margin (approximately an extra 2.5" or 3") and in ALL CAPS. I like to bold them as well, because it makes the speaker stand out, but that's totally optional.

Dialogue follows the name of the speaker on the next line, single-spaced and running margin to margin.

In the case of a musical, song lyrics are in ALL CAPS and run margin to margin like dialogue (though some people will indent them slightly).

Stage directions go on their own line and in parentheses, indented an extra 2" on the left side (3.5" from the left edge of the paper). If they happen while one character is speaking (and the same character is still speaking afterward), single space between the stage directions and the dialogue. If stage directions happen between two speeches, double space between the stage directions and both the previous dialogue and the next speaker's name. Note that some writers indent these internal stage directions (sometimes called a character stage direction or a parenthetical because they usually modify that character's dialogue) less than action, but that's a personal choice. I keep them all the same, because I like the consistent eye-line.

Some writers like to capitalize character names every time they appear in the stage directions. Personally, I like to do what they do in film: only capitalize the name the first time a character appears, thus announcing that there's a new character in the play.

When it's finally time to submit, your script should be three-hole punched (though ten-minute plays are usually just stapled in the upper left-hand corner). You can either use a cover with built-in fasteners, or use brads (a.k.a. roundhead fasteners, usually #6 for a full-length script) and a sheet of cardstock on either side for a cover. Whatever you do for a cover, don't use anything fancy or put art on it, and use a soft cover: remember that literary offices have huge stacks of scripts, and thick, hard covers take up too much space. If you use brads, do what the film people do and use a brad in the top and bottom holes, leaving the middle hole open.

What Is the Running Time of My Play?

The rule of thumb is often given as a minute per page, but the reality is that it's probably a little longer than that—closer to a minute and a half. But it depends on your writing. If a page consists only of a flurry of one-liners meant to be delivered at a brisk pace, that page could take less than a minute. My play *Pepperoni Apocalypse* is like that. In manuscript form, the play is fifteen and a half pages, so one would think that it would run between fifteen and twenty minutes. But because of the rapid-fire dialogue, if properly directed, it should run just under ten minutes. On the other hand, a page with several long speeches (or that is entirely taken up by a monologue) could run two minutes or even longer. Similarly, if there is a great deal of action written into the stage directions, that action could take up considerable stage time without necessarily taking up much space on the page. The opposite is also true: lengthy descriptions, particularly at the opening of scenes (for example, setting up what is on stage when the scene begins), take up much more space on the page than they do time on the stage.

Play Formats Outside of the United States

Before we go to look at some samples, it should be said that if you live outside of the United States, the standard format may be different. In Australia and New Zealand, the format is the same as in the United States, but in Canada, France and the United Kingdom, the format looks more like the published play format I illustrated on the previous page. The name of the character speaking is flush left and in all

CAPS—and may be in boldface to increase visibility. The dialogue follows on the same line, indented 1.5" to 2", enough for there to be sufficient white space so that it's easily readable. Description and action stage directions go on a separate line, single-spaced, usually indented .5" to 1" and italicized, whereas character stage directions (e.g. line readings) go on the same line as the dialogue, italicized and in parentheses. Double-space after dialogue or stage directions (except for character stage directions within the dialogue).

And now for some samples of American manuscript format...

Sample Title Page

The title starts about halfway down the page. In the case of *Dear Chuck*, the play was a commission, so there's a special note about that—otherwise, just put the title and your name. Below you'll find my address, phone number, email and a draft number (in case there are multiple drafts, the draft number avoids confusion).

DEAR CHUCK
Jonathan Dorf

Originally commissioned and developed
by the Choate Rosemary Hall Summer Arts Conservatory

1234 Playwright Street
Playwright City, CA 12345
555-555-5555
jon@playwrightstreet.com
DRAFT 1.6

Sample Cast of Characters Page

This is from *The White Pages.* Note that it contains both cast and setting information. Everyone does this page a little differently. As long as you're in the proverbial ballpark, you'll be fine.

List of Characters

ROBERT, bookish thirtysomething insurance adjuster
NANCY, same age, and far too nice to be true
TOTO, college age and not the sharpest tack in the box
THE OTHER CUSTOMERS, played by the same actress
        MOLLY, the First Customer
        POLLY, the Second Customer
        DOLLY, the Third Customer

To increase the cast size, the Customers may be played by different actresses.

Notes on the Set

While it's important to create the idea of the bookstore, the set may be as surreal or as suggested as necessary, given the budget or limitations of the production.

Sample Song Information Page

In a musical, this page would follow the Cast of Characters page (in a non-musical, you'd just go right to Page One). Again, you'll see some variation in format, but typically you'll see the song title on the left, and then in the right-hand column will be the characters who sing in it. (This is the actual song list from my musical *Day One*.)

List of Songs

Act I

"Day One"	The Cast
"A Hole in the Wall"	Jake, Stanley, Wannabes
"This Place This Time"	Stanley, Stella, Jake
"Muhammad Ali"	Skeeter
"The Solution is Clear"	Erika, Skeeter, Wannabes
"The Solution is Clear" (reprise)	Erika, Skeeter, Blaise
"Fifteen Minutes"	Thyme, Ensemble
"Melt Into Me"	Helen
"A Good Boy is Hard to Find, and a Good Man is Downright Impossible"	Wannabes
"Out Past Infinity"	Blaise
"Don't Let it Splatter"	Helen, Jake, Stanley, Stella, Skeeter

Act II

"Locker Room Blues/Year-Long Limbo"	Skeeter, The Cast
"New School Order"	Erika, Wannabes
"Lost Sheep"	Helen, Jake, Stanley, Stella
"I Hate Stanley"	Stella
"Sand"	Thyme, Jake
"Come on, Jake"	Wannabes
"Sturdy and Strong"	Blaise, Jake
"I Hate Stanley" (reprise)	Helen, Wannabes
"In a Heartbeat"	Stanley, Stella, Helen
"The Dance/Finale"	The Cast

Sample Page One from a Non-Musical Play (American manuscript format)

The opening stage direction, sometimes called the "at-rise description" (discussed in Chapter 6), can either be indented as below, or it can be indented the same distance as the other stage directions. Act and Scene headings only apply as necessary; not every play has acts or even scenes. Font size here is reduced to fit the page.

ACT I

SCENE 1

> *(Author's Note: It is crucial that the set and staging allow the play to run continuously. Elizabethan staging, with the stage separated into playing areas, is the most plausible solution.* Somewhere in America not so long ago. A steamy mid-afternoon the week before Labor Day. CHARLIE, 14 or 15 years old, sits on a suitcase on a sidewalk and holds an ice cream cone. He's sturdy and has the spark of a natural leader. A pile of luggage surrounds him. He taps his foot and looks as if he's waiting for someone. Beat. Enter HUGO, a year younger and a little smaller than Charlie, brainy but not unathletic.)

CHARLIE

Seen my parents?

(Hugo shakes his head and wipes his sweaty face on his shirt.)

My Dad says he's gotta' stop by the bank, and to get him an ice cream cone.

HUGO

How come he still likes ice cream?

CHARLIE

He says wait for him with our stuff. His cone's gonna' melt.

HUGO

I'll eat it.

Sample Page from a Musical (American manuscript format)

Here, lyrics and spoken dialogue mix on a page. Some people indent lyrics (perhaps .5"), but I think the CAPS set them off plenty without having to do so. Again, the font size is reduced to fit the page.

SKEETER
(throws himself on the ground)

Don't kill me!

ERIKA

If you don't have a pass, you're late to first period.

SKEETER
(holds out his wallet without necessarily looking up)

Here. Take my money.

ERIKA

What are your impressions of your new school so far?

SKEETER
(beat)

What?

ERIKA

Sorry—you're a freshman, right?
(to herself)
Speak slowly. Use small words.
(to Skeeter, speaking stereotypically to a foreigner)
What do you think of your new school so far?
(beat)
Let's go—the bell rang five minutes ago, and you don't have a hall pass.

(Erika pulls Skeeter to his feet, but he breaks away.)

SKEETER

THE BELL HAS RUNG
MY BELL'S BEEN RUNG
THREE TIMES ALREADY THIS MORNING
OR WAS IT FOUR—I'M HARDLY THROUGH THE DOOR
AND I CAN'T TAKE IT ANYMORE

I DIDN'T ASK TO BE IN HONORS MATH
OR FOR THAT GIRL TO CHOP MY LUNCH IN HALF
AND LEAVE ME FOR DEAD
WITH THE FOOD CHAIN WRAPPED AROUND MY HEAD

Appendix B

THE BUSINESS OF PLAYWRITING

Being a playwright isn't just about writing good plays. It's about writing good plays and then getting them produced—because what's the point of writing a great play that no one ever sees? When you write a play that someone wants to produce, a whole new learning experience begins. You have certain rights, and it's important to know what they are. Even when there is no money involved (and usually for young playwrights there isn't), there are still many important rights that you have, and those rights need to be respected. The best way to do that is with a clear contract or letter of agreement between you and the producer.

First off, you may be wondering...

Should I Copyright My Play?

Plays are copyrighted from the moment you write them, officially registered or not. But only by registering your play with the Register of Copyrights at the Library of Congress (or your equivalent national registry if you're outside the US) do you have any legal protection. In other words, if someone steals your play and you need to sue them for copyright infringement, you need that official registration to proceed.

Realistically, almost no one steals plays because, unlike screenplays, there's very little to be gained financially. Most plays don't earn much—if any—money. But if you're planning to submit your play around, it's not a bad idea to get it registered, or at least to do so prior to its first production. You can visit http://www.loc.gov/copyright to download a Form PA (performing arts), the form required to copyright plays, musicals, screenplays, etc.

At printing, the cost of registration was $30, and while you won't receive your official certificate of copyright for some months after you apply (this must be done by US mail), rest assured that your play is registered from the date they receive it.

One little known fact about copyright that can save you a boatload of money is that you can copyright several plays at once as a collection. For example, I took a group of my ten-minute plays, called them *Dorf Short Shorts*, and copyrighted them as a collection for a single $30 fee. Similarly, I took a group of my one-acts and copyrighted them together as *Dorf Knee Shorts* (being slightly longer in running time than the *Short Shorts*).

The Playwright's Bill of Rights

No one can perform your copyrighted play without obtaining your permission first. This applies to school productions, productions that don't charge admission, forensics or similar non-commercial ventures. This also applies to public readings. The problem is that many people (particularly at schools, it seems) don't understand how copyrights, permissions and royalties work.

The Dramatists Guild of America is the professional organization of playwrights, composers and lyricists in the United States. The main mission of the Guild is to protect the rights of its members (and of all writers for the stage), and as a student, you're eligible to join at a discounted rate. Visit http://www.dramatistsguild.com for more information. Anyone who is serious about writing plays should join the Guild or its foreign equivalent. If you're a Guild member, you get access to contracts that spell out your rights. Just what are they?

You own your play. It doesn't matter who produces it: you own it before, during and after the production. They're just renting it for a while. This is a major difference between plays and screenplays, because while plays are always the property of the playwright, screenplays are usually bought outright by the production company. Of course, screenwriters usually make much more money, but that's because they're giving up their ownership rights.

No one can change a word of what you have written without your permission. Period. That means no cuts, no additions—no changes of any kind unless you say OK. This applies to dialogue, stage directions and character genders. I once pulled a reading of a play of mine at a college when I wasn't convinced the director was going to follow this rule. Now before you go ballistic on a director for ignoring a "pause," you as the writer are responsible for exercising common sense. To me, changing a stage direction is when you write that "Ben exits" and the director keeps him on stage.

All changes to the script become your property. If you allow a change in your script based on someone else's suggestion, the change becomes YOUR property. No one should get partial ownership of your play because they suggested you "try it this way." But make sure you get this in writing. *Rent* went into several years of legal battles because of the lack of a written agreement between the late Jonathan Larson and the dramaturg who helped him shape the script.

You are allowed to attend all rehearsals and performances (for free). You may not want to or be able to, but you are entitled to. Of course, you must conduct yourself professionally at all times. This means not trying to direct the play in rehearsal. Have a question or problem? Take the director aside during a break in rehearsal (unless you and the director have agreed upon this in advance, you should NEVER communicate directly with the actors or crew other than to exchange pleasantries, nor should you start arguing with the director in front of the actors or crew). If you feel that the director isn't listening, talk to the producer or whichever person is ultimately in charge.

Personally, I like to attend the read-through and then go away for a while and let the actors and directors stumble around the script without me. They need that time to try things out and make mistakes without worrying that the playwright is there watching their every move. (Yes, most actors get nervous and self-conscious with the playwright around.) And frankly, watching directors work on staging is boring. So I let them work on the play for a while, and then I come back later in the rehearsal process. The added advantage of working that way is that I get to look at the play with fresh eyes, which is hard to do if you've been there every single day.

If the play is new or still in development, there's a good chance you may be rewriting it during production. You'll want to discuss with the director how bringing in rewrites is going to work. Chances are you'll give the pages to the director to distribute to the actors, and at a certain point, the script will be "locked": you'll stop giving them changes so that the actors can actually memorize.

Be aware that no matter how you imagine the play or hear it in your head, it's not going to come out that way in production—not even if you direct it yourself. Our imaginations never translate exactly. But instead of panicking, try keeping an open mind: in a good production, your play can actually become better than you imagined.

You should receive a copy of the program and any other publicity materials issued by the producing group, as well as any reviews and newspaper coverage, should they exist (it's unlikely that a young playwrights festival/production will be reviewed, but just in case...). Some productions are very good about doing this, but unfortunately, often they'll promise you the moon before the production, and then afterward, they won't return your emails or calls. Not much you can do about it, so just move on to the next thing.

What About Royalties?

At the young playwrights level, most productions don't pay royalties, because you're still considered to be learning, and the production is its own reward: it's an educational experience. And if your own high school or college does your play (unless it's published), don't expect them to pay you—again, it's about your learning process.

But once you get out in the "real world," whenever a play gets produced, the playwright gets paid a royalty. Think of it as a rental fee. It doesn't matter if the production isn't charging admission or isn't making a profit, though there are times when you might want to waive royalties: for example, in a classroom setting (regular school productions are a major royalty market, and should always pay royalties), or a one-time charity/benefit performance. Some playwrights, in the case of a benefit, will donate their royalties back to the charity, because they don't want to set the precedent of not receiving royalties at all. Why is not charging royalties a bad idea under most circumstances? Because a royalty says that a writer's work is of value, and when you give that up, you're sending the message that you don't think your work is worth anything. And not only that, but it makes it that much harder for other writers to collect their royalties. Is that really the message you want to send? Yes, you want your work to be seen, but do you really want it to be seen at the expense of your rights and dignity?

Before departing the Royalties section, one tricky issue is that of forensics, a competition in which high school or college students, solo or in pairs ("duets"), will perform either a short play or an excerpt from a longer one, dramatically interpreting it in front of judges. It's not a production, and it can be good exposure for you to let them use your play. But should you get paid nothing when you end up providing them with material that gets used over and over during the course of their competition season? What Brooklyn Publishers—one of my publishers and one that does a large business in scripts for forensics—does is charge for the copies of the scripts, but not a production royalty. I've taken to using a similar arrangement with my unpublished scripts. That way, they're paying something (acknowledging the value of your work), but you're not charging a full production royalty for something that's not a production.

What If Someone Wants to Publish My Play?

Young playwrights who win contests (particularly the big national competitions) sometimes get offers of publication. Or sometimes young writers just submit through traditional channels (i.e. they send in their plays just like anybody else) and get an offer. Publication is very different from production. While technically you still own your play, the publisher will administer it for you. What does this mean? It means that when someone wants to produce your published play, instead of contacting you for permission, they'll contact the publisher. The publisher will then take care of sending out copies of the play and of making sure the royalties have been paid.

Why get your play published? In a word, marketing. Publishers have access to a much larger market than do individual playwrights. Each year, play publishing companies mail their script catalogues to thousands of schools and theatres companies, their websites attract many prospective producers and they generate visibility by attending conferences and festivals. Your work has a chance to gain a great deal of exposure. Sounds great, right?

Ultimately, publishing is usually a good thing. But keep in mind that some things change when you get a play published. The publisher takes over the licensing of productions, so you'll often be out of the loop (except for big professional productions, where you will still be significantly involved). They'll now share your royalties and send you a check and a statement once or twice a year (some companies allow you to track your sales on the web, but that's still a developing technology). Deals on performance royalties range anywhere from a 50-50 split (I'd never take anything less than that) to as much as 80-20 in your favor, depending on the company and your level of experience or clout. You'll also typically get 10% on script sales (so if they sell 10 scripts at $6 each, you'll get $6). But it's better to get 50 or 60% of something than to get 100% of nothing—right?

Before signing with any publisher, find out how much marketing they do (printed catalogues, visiting festivals, etc) to make sure that you're satisfied that your play is going to get wide exposure. Just because a play gets published is no guarantee that it will get lots of (or any) productions. So don't stop marketing it on your own—whether that means taking advantage of the marketing opportunities of the internet (there are numerous sites that will allow you to list your plays for free), doing postcard mailings to venues that might be appropriate, or getting involved with local theatres to get an "in." You still need to be your own advocate.

Keep in mind that publishers tend to be most interested in plays that have already had some success, so I'd worry about getting some productions first before you try to get published. Walk before you run.

Appendix C

SUBMISSION RESOURCES AND OPPORTUNITIES

Submission Resources

You've worked hard, writing and rewriting, and you've written a great play. It won't matter if you don't know where to send it. A book that most playwrights own is *The Dramatists Sourcebook*, which comes out every other September (the last one came out in 2004) and lists nearly 1000 submission opportunities, including a healthy number for young playwrights. You can order it directly from The Writers Store at http://www.writersstore.com or through any major bookstore chain (either online or in person).

A similar resource is the *Resource Guide* of the Dramatists Guild of America (http://www.dramatistsguild.com), which comes out annually. As mentioned earlier, the Dramatists Guild is the national organization for playwrights, composers and lyricists, formed to protect our rights. Not only does your annual membership come with a copy of the Resource Guide, but you also get the bimonthly magazine *The Dramatist*, access to free legal advice (for example, if someone offers you a production contract and you want a lawyer to look it over), your own web page on the Guild site and much, much more. There's a student membership, and I highly recommend that you join.

Online, you'll find a variety of resources, though most of them are oriented toward adult playwrights. But keep your eyes open, because you never know. Here are a few possibilities:

American Theater Web (http://www.americantheaterweb.com) has an index of links to pretty much every American theatre with a website, plus a callboard where producers occasionally post calls for scripts (the callboard seems to have fallen into disuse). It's a great place to research what kinds of plays a theatre may produce.

Playwrights on the Web (http://www.stageplays.com), run by Paul Thain in the UK, has both a front section where most of its opportunities get posted and a bulletin board where a few others show up as well. Be aware that the bulletin board is an open forum, which means that the posts there are not always appropriate for young people.

Playwriting Opportunities (http://www.playwritingopportunities.com) has been one of the best sources of links to playwriting contests and submission opportunities around, though it has been on hiatus for some time, and its future isn't 100 percent clear.

Another site along the same lines as Playwriting Opportunities is The Burry Man Writers Center (http://www.burryman.com), which also features, in addition to links to contests, links to helpful writing reference sources.

Send an email to young_playwrights-subscribe@yahoogroups.com to join the discussion group (aka list-serv) I moderate—it's a place where young playwrights and those who teach them can discuss issues specific to young writers.

Send an email to playsandplaywrights-subscribe@yahoogroups.com to join a discussion group (aka list-serv) whose membership includes hundreds of playwrights of all ages, though most are adults and some are quite accomplished.

Absolutely Theatre (http://groups.msn.com/AbsolutelyTheatre) is an MSN discussion forum with multiple bulletin boards, including one that is specifically for playwrights.

En Avant (http://p202.ezboard.com/benavantplaywrights) is another bulletin board where many submission opportunities get posted.

The following three resources are specifically international:
http://www.ozscript.org (Australia)
http://www.playwrightsguild.com (Canada)
http://www.britishtheatreguide.info (United Kingdom)

Contests and Calls for Scripts

There are a host of playwriting contests and submission opportunities designed specifically for young writers. Winning them can be a great experience. Several of my students won the Blank Theatre competition in Los Angeles, and they received workshop productions with professional actors and directors, professional writers serving as mentors, and all kinds of "good fuss." They had a wonderful time. Many contests are like that, providing lots of nurturing to those who win (and even supportive critiques to those who enter in some cases). I'm all for them.

You may be thinking, "Why can't I submit to the same contests as adult writers?" There's nothing stopping you, but the reality is that you'd be competing against writers who are much older and much more experienced. Sending out scripts requires time and usually money (unless you can submit online, you're going to have to make a copy of the play and pay for an envelope and postage), so why waste both when the odds are strongly against you? Take advantage of the fact that you're a young playwright and have lots of contests designed specifically for writers your age. There will be plenty of time to compete with professional writers when you're older.

Note about Listings: While these listings and links were accurate at the time of publication, contests and companies can often change without warning. I take no responsibility for any changes in the listings here, nor does any listing constitute an endorsement of any kind. In other words, all submissions are at your own risk. If you find a broken link (it's not uncommon for links to change, for example, when a company redesigns its website), please email me at jon@youngplaywrights101.com.

Note about Entry Fees: I am against entry/reading fees in general, but I am particularly against them for young writers. Postage, copying and envelopes cost enough without adding a fee to them, and entry fees discriminate against talented young writers who may not be able to afford this extra expense. To the best of my knowledge, none of the contests listed charge fees—if you find that one of them does, please let me know.

The listings below are divided into contests for American high school and younger students, American college students, students of all ages outside the United States, and contests without any geographic limitations. In all cases, it's up to you to research their guidelines and see if you qualify.

Opportunities for High School and Younger Students in the United States

Alabama Shakespeare Festival (March 13)
http://www.asfeducation.com/playwrights/index.html
Open to Alabama high school students in grades 9-12.

All Children's Theatre Youth Playwriting Competition (December 8)
http://www.actinri.org/PlaywritingFestival.htm
Open to Rhode Island high school students.

Arena Stage Student Ten-Minute Competition (deadline TBA)
http://www.arenastage.org/education/playwrightsproject
Open to students from the District of Columbia, the City of Alexandria, or one of the following counties: Loudoun, Prince Georges, Prince William, Montgomery, Fairfax or Arlington. Students must be in grades 6-12.

Arlington Children's Theater Young Playwrights (September 1)
http://act.arlington.ma.us/PWContest
Open to all. 18 years old or younger.

Baker's Plays (Jan 30 for 2005)
http://bakersplays.com (click on Play Submissions)
Open to all high school students.

Blank Theatre Young Playwrights Festival (March 15)
http://www.youngplaywrights.com
Open to anyone 19 years old or younger.

California Young Playwrights Project (June 1)
http://www.playwrightsproject.com/con.html
Open to residents of California under the age of 19.

CenterStage Young Playwrights Festival (February 17)
http://www.centerstage.com (click on Community)
Open to students in Maryland.

City Theatre Company Young Playwright's Contest (April 15)
http://www.citytheatrecompany.org (click on Education)
Open to students in Western Pennsylvania in grades 7-12.

Curious Theatre Company (see website for details)
http://www.curioustheatre.org/newwork/newvoices.htm
Their New Voices program is open to young playwrights ages 15-21
and offers play development (culminating in public staged readings)
and instruction with seasoned professional playwrights, with all
participants receiving full scholarships. The company is based in
Denver, though not all past participants have been from Colorado.

Delaware Theatre Company, Delaware Young Playwrights Festival
(deadline TBA)
http://www.delawaretheatre.org (click on Education)
Open to Delaware students. Check website for more information.

Dobama Theatre's Marilyn Bianchi Kids' Playwriting Festival (see website for deadlines)
http://www.dobama.org/bianchi.html
Open to Cuyahoga County (OH) students in grades 1-12. Deadlines are staggered according to student grade level during February and March.

Florida Stage (December 16)
http://www.floridastage.org/young_play.shtml
Open to any Palm Beach County student in grades K-12.

Geva Theatre (winter deadline)
http://www.gevatheatre.org/onstage/playwrights.php
Open to Rochester-area writers, ages 13-18. For more information, send an email to gevatalk@gevatheatre.org.

Gorilla Theatre, Young Dramatists Project (February 18)
http://www.gorilla-theatre.com/ydp_2005_guidelines.html
Open to middle or high school students in Hillsborough or Pinellas County (FL).

Innovative Stages' Young Playwrights Competition (March 15)
http://www.innovativestages.com/Young Playwrights.htm
Open to residents of Westchester County (NY), grades 9-12.

Lebanon Community Theater's Playwriting Contest (April 30)
http://www.lct.cc/PlayWriteContest.htm
Open to playwrights of all ages and experience. All plays must be written only for this contest and must not exceed 20 minutes of production time. Check website for more information.

The Midwest High School Playwriting Competition (March 25)
http://www.indstate.edu/theatre/mhspc/Guidelines.htm
Open to high school students in Illinois, Indiana, Iowa, Kansas, Kentucky, Michigan, Minnesota, Missouri, Nebraska, North Dakota, Ohio, South Dakota and Wisconsin. Students who are new to playwriting are especially encouraged to write a play and submit it to the competition.

New South Young Playwrights Festival Contest (deadline TBA)
http://www.horizontheatre.com/education&outreach.htm
Sponsored by Horizon Theatre Company, this festival for southern young writers has divisions for middle school and high school (as well as college) playwrights. Check their website for details.

Orange Tree Theatre Company (ongoing)
http://meltingpot.fortunecity.com/stark/250/orangetree.html
This theatre company in Ithaca (NY) is run by teens for teens.

Pegasus Players (deadline TBA)
http://www.pegasusplayers.org
This is open to Chicago residents, but while the contest still exists, there's little info online, so you'll have to contact the theatre for details.

Philadelphia Young Playwrights (May 16)
http://phillyyoungplaywrights.org
Open to high school students in the Philadelphia area.

Playwrights Theatre of New Jersey, New Jersey Young Playwrights Contest (January 26 for high school; February 16 for junior high and elementary)
http://www.ptnj.org/NJWP/NJWP_d1c.htm
Open to New Jersey students in grades 4-12.

Princeton University Ten-Minute Play Contest (March 1)
http://www.princeton.edu/~visarts/tenminply.htm
Open to any student in grade 11 during the current academic year.

San Francisco Young Playwrights Festival (December 16)
http://www.sfyoungplaywrights.org
Open to high school students in San Francisco.

Scholastic Writing Awards (deadlines vary according to region)
http://www.scholastic.com/artandwritingawards/enter.htm
Open to students enrolled in grades 7-12.

Shenandoah Valley Regional Playwright's Festival (January 13)
http://www.waysidetheatre.org/Education/youngplaywrights.htm
Open to students under the age of 19 on the submission deadline, residing in Virginia or West Virginia (see entry instructions for specific counties of residence).

Syracuse Stage (February 14)
http://www.syracusestage.org/education_ypf.html
Open to Central New York students.

TADA! (January 4)
http://www.tadatheater.com/teens/Default.asp
Open to all. To enter the "young writers" category, entrants must be 19 or under, though there is also a category for writers over 19. Separate instructions for musicals.

Thespian Playworks (February 17)
http://www.edta.org/rehearsal_hall/thespian_playworks.asp
Open to any active member of the Thespian Society who is a high school student during the current school year.

Vermont Young Playwright's Project (deadline TBA)
http://www.vtstage.org/vtyoung.html
Open to middle and high school students from Vermont. Scripts selected through school workshops. Contact them for more information.

VSA Playwright Discovery Program (April 15)
http://www.vsarts.org/x1548.xml
Open to entrants 21 and under. Plays must deal with some aspect of disability.

Waterfront Ensemble/ New Jersey Dramatists (February 1)
http://www.waterfrontensemble.org/
Open to all students from New Jersey. Plays and monologues should be no more than 20 minutes in length.

Write A Play! NYC School Playwriting Contest (April 1)
http://www.youngplaywrights.org/NYCcontest.htm
Open to all New York City students.

Young Playwrights Festival National Playwriting Contest (December 1)
http://www.youngplaywrights.org/nationalcontest.htm
Open to all entrants ages 18 or younger.

Competitions for College Students in the United States

Marc A. Klein Playwriting Award (December 1)
ksg@case.edu
Department of Theater Arts, Case Western Reserve University, 10900 Euclid Avenue, Cleveland, OH 44106-7077, c/o Ron Wilson, Chair, Reading Committee. Open to American college students.

New South Young Playwrights Festival Contest (deadline TBA)
http://www.horizontheatre.com/education&outreach.htm
Sponsored by Horizon Theatre Company, this festival is open to southern college writers. Check their website or contact them for details.

Wichita State University (February 15)
http://finearts.wichita.edu/performing/contest.asp
Open to all undergraduate and graduate students enrolled at any college or university.

Competitions Outside the United States

Magnus Theatre (deadline TBA)
http://www.magnus.on.ca/category/21
Open to residents of Northern Ontario (Canada), ages 12-19. Contact them for submission details.

New Zealand Young Playwrights' Competition (December 6)
http://www.playmarket.org.nz/comp_home.php
Open to New Zealand residents ages 16-22.

Sydney Theatre Company's Young Playwrights' Award (August 5)
http://www.sydneytheatre.com.au/content.asp?cID=51
Open to Australian residents of NSW or the ACT 19 years or under.

Under 20 for Under 20's Competition/Tarragon Theatre (January 17)
http://www.tarragontheatre.com/education_under20.php
Open to Ontario (Canada) residents under the age of 20 as of the contest deadline.

Open to All

Fledgling Films (ongoing for production in July)
http://www.fledglingfilms.com/summer.html
Solicits teen and pre-teen written plays, screenplays, and short stories to be produced as short films at the Fledgling Films Summer Institute. Accepts national and international submissions, with a strong preference toward works written primarily in English. Writers receive small honorarium, an invitation to be involved in the filming process and a copy of the finished film. Ideal script is 10-30 pages. Submit to: Fledgling Films, 949 Somers Road, Barnet, Vermont 05821, USA. Send SASE for return of materials. E-mail kcp@pshift.com for more information.

International Student Playscript Competition (November 30)
http://www.nsdf.org.uk/
Must be a current student or recent graduate. See website for details.

Appendix D

QUERY AND COVER LETTERS

When you submit a play to a theatre or a contest, you rarely just send the script. Usually you send a letter with it. Letters come in different varieties. There's what we call the query letter, which is what you send when you're trying to convince them to read your script (a query letter is often accompanied by a synopsis and/or sample pages, depending on what the theatre wants). And then there are two kinds of cover letters, one for when they've already asked for your script (a solicited script), and another when they haven't (an unsolicited script). Each letter is a little different, but keep reading for an example of each, as well as advice on how to write letters that work.

You should always find out what a theatre's submission guidelines are before sending them anything. There is nothing more annoying than having someone submit a 30-page play when you're only looking for 10-minute pieces, or receiving a full script when you've said that you only accept query letters accompanied by a synopsis and sample pages (if they ask for sample pages and don't tell you otherwise, send the first 10 pages). Some theatres only accept scripts submitted by literary agents or with a professional recommendation (usually from a literary manager or artistic director of another theatre company), so if you don't have one of those, best to look for other opportunities. Most theatres will, however, accept a query letter, and some accept unsolicited scripts.

In the case of a query letter or the cover letter for an unsolicited script, this letter is your first contact with the theatre. It's your opportunity to show them that you take this seriously, and that you can write—

yes, your letter is the first place they will judge your writing. It's crucial that it be well-written and free of typographical errors.

Never write a letter longer than a page—no one wants to read that much. I follow a simple, three-paragraph formula. The first paragraph is a little about what I'm sending, and that it's a good fit for their organization. The second paragraph tells them about me. The third paragraph tells them how to reach me and thanks them for considering my work. Keep it simple and modest. Don't tell them how funny your comedy is, how you think your play will change the world or what a great writer you are. That makes you sound arrogant and amateurish, and I've been in theatre literary offices where such letters have been held up and laughed at. That is not a good way to introduce yourself to an overworked literary staff.

Before we get into the samples, a few notes on what to send with your letters and scripts:

Sending Query Letters

When sending a query, include either a self-addressed stamped envelope (SASE) or a self-addressed stamped postcard (SASP), or you will likely never get a response. Sometimes you don't get one anyway; that's life. Response time varies from almost immediate to well over a year. Don't expect to get your synopsis or sample pages back. I use a postcard and give them three boxes to check: "Send me the script," "Send me the script, but wait until _____," or "Other," below which I include blank lines for an explanation of what they mean. I don't give them an easy way to check "no." The hope is that if they check "Other," they'll tell me why. Sometimes they do, which can be useful in future submissions to that company.

Sending Scripts

With script submissions, I enclose a business-size SASE. It's not cost-effective to spend three dollars (or more) on postage to get back a potentially dog-eared, coffee-stained script—I'll probably have rewritten it in the year it might take to get a response. Yes, responses to a full script usually take anywhere from a month or two to a year or two. Be patient. Very, very patient. As I've said before, go write something else so that you're not sitting on your hands waiting.

Sample Query Letter (font reduced to fit the page)

555 Writer's Alley
New York, NY 10003
August 12, 2005

John Smith
Artistic Director
Pilgrim Theater Company
525 Puritan Way
Plymouth, MA 02156

Dear Mr. Smith:

Enclosed for your consideration please find a synopsis and sample pages from *Milk and Cookies*. *Milk and Cookies* is about Margaret Nancy Reagan Ballmoth, who becomes a fugitive when her children poison the cookies they give the teller at a bank's drive-through window. She meets up with Bruce, a man on the run from "milk," which he believes to be the industrial in the military-industrial complex. It runs approximately 100 minutes, has a cast of 4 and has minimal set and technical requirements. Enjoy.

Milk and Cookies was a winner of the 2005 Writer's Alley Young Playwrights Contest, and it received a staged reading through the contest this spring. Another play, *Tea and Biscuits*, was produced locally at Writer's Alley High School as part of the Writer's Alley Spring Fling It on the Wall and Hope No One Gets Splattered Festival. I am a member of the Dramatists Guild and the Writer's Alley Young Playwrights Workshop. [Some groups may ask for a resume, in which case you can add "Enclosed for your convenience is a resume" here.]

Enclosed is a stamped postcard to facilitate a reply at your earliest convenience, and you can also reach me by phone at 555-555-5555 or via email at jondorf@writersalley.com. Thank you for your attention, and I look forward to sending you the full script.

Best,

Jon Dorf

Sample Unsolicited Script Letter (font reduced to fit the page)

555 Writer's Alley
New York, NY 10003
August 12, 2005

John Smith
Artistic Director
Pilgrim Theater Company
525 Puritan Way
Plymouth, MA 02156

Dear Mr. Smith:

Enclosed for your consideration please find *Milk and Cookies*. *Milk and Cookies* is about Margaret Nancy Reagan Ballmoth, who becomes a fugitive when her children poison the cookies they give the teller at a bank's drive-through window. She meets up with Bruce, a man on the run from "milk," which he believes to be the industrial in the military-industrial complex. It runs approximately 100 minutes, has a cast of 4 and has minimal set and technical requirements. Enjoy.

Milk and Cookies was a winner of the 2005 Writer's Alley Young Playwrights Contest, and it received a staged reading through the contest this spring. Another play, *Tea and Biscuits*, was produced locally at Writer's Alley High School as part of the Writer's Alley Spring Fling It on the Wall and Hope No One Gets Splattered Festival. I am a member of the Dramatists Guild and the Writer's Alley Young Playwrights Workshop. [If they ask for a resume, you can add "Enclosed for your convenience is a resume" here.]

Enclosed is a SASE to facilitate a reply at your earliest convenience (recycle the script if it's not for you), and you can also reach me at 555-555-5555. Thank you for your interest in my work, and I look forward to getting your thoughts on *Milk and Cookies*.

Regards,

Jon Dorf

Sample Solicited Script Letter

They've read your query letter, or perhaps they've heard about your play because of a contest win or through someone at another theatre. In any case, they want to read your script. Now what? Try this letter on for size.

555 Writer's Alley
New York, NY 10003
August 12, 2005

John Smith
Artistic Director
Pilgrim Theater Company
525 Puritan Way
Plymouth, MA 02156

Dear Mr. Smith:

Thank you for requesting *Milk and Cookies*, which I enclose. Enjoy.

Enclosed is a SASE to facilitate a reply at your earliest convenience (recycle the script if it's not for you), and you can also reach me at 555-555-5555. Thanks so much for your interest in my work, and I look forward to getting your thoughts on the play.

Best,

Jon Dorf

Notice how short the letter is. They want it, so here it is. Sometimes I like to mention any news about my writing (e.g. a recent award or production) or current projects I'm working on. If you choose to do that, the ideal place is between the opening and closing paragraphs.

Appendix E

SUGGESTED READING LIST

If you are going to be a serious playwright (or actor, director, designer, etc), you need to be a serious play reader. Even if you can't afford to be a frequent theatergoer or own a large book collection, everyone can afford the library.

I've made a list of plays I think you ought to read. The list includes plays of different periods and writers who have different backgrounds and writing styles. It's not complete, and it's just my opinion. I've tried to select, for each major dramatist, at least one or two representative plays (in parentheses you'll find other recommended plays by that playwright). Some are difficult reading, and some (particularly the contemporary material) may have adult language or content. All can be handled, at least on some level, by a high school student with a little determination.

One thing to remember before plunging forward is that we often imitate our influences, at least for a little while. In other words, if you read a couple of Beckett plays early in your development, I'd be willing to bet that the next few pieces you write will read like Beckett—until you get his work out of your system (I admit I went through a Beckett/Ionesco period). So after you read that Beckett play, go out and read Arthur Miller or Shakespeare or Chekhov or Marsha Norman. Keep it varied, and as you swill all of these different styles around in the melting pot of your mind, your own style will develop.

The list:

Classical
Eumenides (or any part of *The Oresteia*) by Aeschylus
Lysistrata by Aristophanes
The Bacchae by Euripides
Medea by Seneca
Antigone by Sophocles (*Oedipus Rex*)

The Elizabethans and Jacobeans
Life is a Dream by Pedro Calderon de la Barca
'Tis Pity She's a Whore by John Ford
Volpone by Ben Jonson
Edward the Second and *Doctor Faustus* by Christopher Marlowe
A Midsummer Night's Dream, Romeo and Juliet and *Richard III* by William Shakespeare. (Pretty much anything by Shakespeare is a good idea, and certainly *Hamlet, King Lear, Macbeth* and *Othello* are worthy additions to this list—just a bit more difficult.)
Fuente Ovejuna by Lope de Vega

Restoration, Seventeenth and Eighteenth Century Classics
She Stoops to Conquer by Oliver Goldsmith
The Miser or *Tartuffe* by Moliere
The Rivals by Richard Sheridan

The "Modern" Dramatists and the Turn of the Twentieth Century
The Cherry Orchard by Anton Chekhov (*Three Sisters*)
Ghosts, A Doll's House and *Hedda Gabler* by Henrik Ibsen
Pygmalion by George Bernard Shaw (*Heartbreak House*)
Miss Julie by August Strindberg
The Importance of Being Earnest by Oscar Wilde

Symbolism
Ubu Roi by Alfred Jarry
The Blue Bird by Maurice Maeterlinck

Twentieth Century American Classics
A Raisin in the Sun by Lorraine Hansberry
You Can't Take It With You by George S. Kaufman and Moss Hart
(*The Man Who Came to Dinner*)
Death of a Salesman by Arthur Miller (*The Crucible, All My Sons*)
Long Day's Journey into Night and *The Iceman Cometh* by Eugene
O'Neill (*Moon for the Misbegotten*)
Our Town by Thornton Wilder
A Streetcar Named Desire and *The Glass Menagerie* by Tennessee
Williams (*Cat on a Hot Tin Roof, Orpheus Descending*)

Twentieth Century European Classics
Mother Courage and *The Caucasian Chalk Circle* by Bertolt Brecht
(*The Good Woman of Szechuan* and *The Threepenny Opera* are
also important plays)
Woyczek by Georg Buchner
Private Lives by Noel Coward
The Visit of the Old Lady by Friedrich Düerrenmatt

The Absurd and the "Postmodern"
Who's Afraid of Virginia Woolf and *The Zoo Story* by Edward Albee
(*Three Tall Women, A Delicate Balance*)
Waiting for Godot by Samuel Beckett (*Endgame, Krapp's Last Tape*)
The Maids by Jean Genet (*The Balcony*)
Rhinoceros by Eugene Ionesco (*The Chairs*)
The Homecoming by Harold Pinter (*Betrayal*)
Six Characters in Search of an Author by Luigi Pirandello (*Henry IV*)
No Exit by Jean Paul Sartre

Eclectic Significant Plays and Playwrights from the 1960s and Later
Cloud Nine by Caryl Churchhill (*Topgirls*)
Fires in the Mirror by Anna Deavere-Smith
Lonely Planet by Steven Dietz (I strongly recommend reading
Ionesco's *The Chairs* first)
Master Harold and the Boys by Athol Fugard
Dutchman by Leroi Jones (aka Amiri Baraka)
Angels in America by Tony Kushner
American Buffalo by David Mamet (*Glengarry Glen Ross*)

Eclectic Significant Plays and Playwrights (cont'd)
Marisol by Jose Rivera
Buried Child and *Curse of the Starving Class* by Sam Shepard
Arcadia by Tom Stoppard (*Rosencrantz and Guildenstern are Dead*)
Fences and *Joe Turner's Come and Gone* by August Wilson (*The Piano Lesson*)

More Top Contemporary Plays and Playwrights (a major work in parentheses)
Lee Blessing (*A Walk in the Woods*), Christopher Durang (*Sister Mary Ignatius Explains It All For You*), Horton Foote (*Young Man from Atlanta*), Maria Irene Fornes (*Fefu and Her Friends*), Brian Friel (*Dancing at Lughnasa*), John Guare (*Six Degrees of Separation*), David Hare (*Skylight*), Beth Henley (*Crimes of the Heart*), Israel Horovitz (*Indian Wants the Bronx*), David Henry Hwang (*M. Butterfly*), William Inge (*Bus Stop*), Moises Kaufman (*The Laramie Project*), Arthur Kopit (*Oh Dad, Poor Dad...*), Suzan-Lori Parks (*Topdog/Underdog*), Marsha Norman (*'Night, Mother*), Joe Orton (*What the Butler Saw*), David Rabe (*The Basic Training of Pavlo Hummel*), Milcha Sanchez-Scott (*Roosters*), Peter Shaffer (*Equus*), Nzotake Shange (*for colored girls who have considered suicide when the rainbow is enuf*), John Patrick Shanley (*The Effect of Gamma Rays on Man in the Moon Marigolds*), Nicky Silver (*Pterodactyls*), Paula Vogel (*How I Learned to Drive*), Alfred Uhry (*Driving Miss Daisy*), Lanford Wilson (*The Rhymers of Eldritch, Burn This*), George C. Wolfe (*The Colored Museum; Bring in 'Da Noise, Bring in 'Da Funk*)

Plays Specifically for Children and Youth
Peter Pan by J.M. Barrie
Reynard the Fox by Arthur Fauquez
The Ice Wolf by Joanna Kraus
Alicia in Wonder Tierra, or I Can't Eat Goat Head by Sylvia Gonzales S.
The Yellow Boad by David Saar
Mother Hicks by Suzan Zeder

Musicals

Assassins, book by John Weidman, music and lyrics by Stephen Sondheim

Big River, book by Roger Miller, music and lyrics by William Hauptman

Chicago by John Kander and Fred Ebb

Children of Eden, book by John Caird, music and lyrics by Stephen Schwartz

A Chorus Line, book by Nicholas Dante and James Kirkwood, music by Marvin Hamlisch, lyrics by Edward Kleban

Falsettos, book by James Lapine and William Finn, music and lyrics by William Finn

Kiss Me Kate, book by Bella and Samuel Spewack, music and lyrics by Cole Porter

My Fair Lady, book and lyrics by Alan Jay Lerner, music by Frederick Loewe

Rent by Jonathan Larson

The Sound of Music, book by Howard Lindsay and Russell Crouse, music by Richard Rodgers, lyrics by Oscar Hammerstein II

Sweeney Todd, music and lyrics by Stephen Sondheim

West Side Story, book by Arthur Laurents, music by Leonard Bernstein, lyrics by Stephen Sondheim

If You've Got a Bit More Time…

These aren't the plays I'd choose to read first, but they're very good and in many cases, very commercially successful, so if you get through the rest of the list, take a look.

Waiting for Lefty by Clifford Odets

Look Back in Anger by John Osborne

The Sisters Rosenzweig by Wendy Wasserstein

Duchess of Malfi by John Webster

Twelve Angry Men by Reginald Rose

Inherit the Wind by Jerome Laurence and Robert E. Lee

Steel Magnolias by Robert Harling